MANUEL MONADE moved to the UK  where he was studying archaeology and art In London, he first qualified as a chef be West End restaurants in the 1980s and 1990s. He joined the original team at St John Restaurant in Smithfield, where head chef and owner Fergus Henderson insisted on having real artisan bread freshly baked in-house for each service. Dan Lepard, the main baker, introduced Manuel to bread making. When Dan left, Manuel took over the small bakery and never returned to working as a chef again. Manuel returned to France to train at *l'Institut National de la Boulangerie Pâtisserie* in Rouen before return- ing to work in London. For many years he worked with Matt Jones at Flourpower City Bakery, before becoming a teacher at Bread Ahead baking school.

Also by Manuel Monade

Breaditation: De-stress by Making Bread (with Caroline Harrison)

ARTISAN BREAD

FROM YOUR
BREAD MACHINE

Quick, easy and excellent bread
at home, including sourdough

Manuel Monade

HEAD START

First published in 2023 by Palazzo Editions Ltd
15 Church Road
London SW13 9HE

www.palazzoeditions.com

Text © 2023 Manuel Monade

Paperback ISBN 9781786751386
eBook ISBN 9781786751584

A CIP catalogue record for this book is available from the British Library.

Every reasonable effort has been made to trace copyright-holders of
material reproduced in this book, but if any have been inadvertently
overlooked the publishers would be glad to hear from them.

Design and typesetting by Danny Lyle

Printed in the UK

10 9 8 7 6 5 4 3 2 1

MIX
Paper | Supporting
responsible forestry
FSC
www.fsc.org
FSC® C171272

Contents

Introduction

Using a bread machine for real artisan baking?! Just suggesting that to the professional bakers I know would certainly make them laugh and provoke endless banter. And if I did this, would my endeavour turn me into some sort of a traitor to real baking?

There is definitely a stigma attached to using a bread machine. As a bakery teacher, many a time have my students introduced themselves at the beginning of a class, almost ashamed of admitting they own such a device, or being very defensive about it. And this got me thinking: should I just consider the whole issue not worth the interest? Is it a waste of time, or should I investigate, experiment and maybe try to find a way of applying the principles of artisan baking to bread machines and see if we can actually make bread that would be just as good as loaves made by traditional techniques?

It is a real challenge, as the whole method used by a bread machine does seem to go against what I see as traditional baking: everything is thrown in, a button is pushed and that's it! Where we usually have a succession of specific and crucial steps in traditional baking – mixing, proving, shaping, proving once again and baking in the oven – with the bread maker, all those steps are crammed into one place, which is very difficult for a professional baker to comprehend and accept. Besides this, the absence of proper steam injection and the impossibility for a bread machine to achieve the higher temperature required for creating a serious crust on a loaf is quite a substantial step back, and the finished result is not particularly attractive to either professional or experienced amateur bakers.

But I can also understand why people are interested in buying a bread machine, because it is such a convenient bit of equipment in our hectic modern-day lives. It also offers you the option to still enjoy baking even if you are removed from most of the process, especially if you can't deal with the stickiness of the dough, or if you can't, for one reason or another, physically knead or shape dough by hand but still want to experience the satisfaction of producing homemade bread.

So what I am proposing in this book is adapting basic artisan baking techniques to a bread machine context in order to help the home baker to produce a flavoursome and nutritious loaf with a little less effort. I'm well aware that I am using my bread machine in a very unusual and unorthodox way here, as in these recipes you will see I add on a few stages to improve the bread machine loaf: pre-fermentation, taking my doughs out of the machine sometimes to finish the kneading by hand, making use of my fridge for extended fermentation for the first and/or second prove, and even loading my tin into the oven to give a better spring to my loaf or to achieve a darker crust. These little tricks do work and don't add too much more effort, and they are well worth doing for a really good, flavoursome homemade loaf.

So let's think outside the pan and bring some artisan expertise to our bread machine!

The Bread Machine

When I started experimenting with my bread machine, the first thing I noticed was it was impossible for it to reach the high temperatures required to achieve a good caramelisation. Most machines will reach 180°C (350°F) maximum, which is quite low for many breads. (In a bakery, most loaves are baked at 230–250°C (446–482°F), while sweet doughs, on the other hand, can be baked at a lower temperature similar to what is achieved in a bread machine. This is worth noting, as enriched doughs do very well in a bread maker.)

Another disadvantage is that the absence of a steaming device in a bread machine means we are missing a vital element during baking: steam delays the coagulation of the gluten and helps the bread to rise before the crust hardens, and it also helps the caramelisation of the natural sugars present on the outside of the loaf, which gives the crust a deeper colour.

To remedy these issues, all the bread recipes that I have read use sugar. While this does, of course, give some lovely colour, the question is: should you really add processed sugar to your daily loaf? We are bombarded with sugar and salt all day long, so we should be able at least to control the quantities we use of these ingredients when cooking at home, which we generally associate with healthy eating and true flavour.

Mixing is another sharp change. In a bread machine, a removable blade rotates at the bottom of the pan, gradually bringing all the ingredients together into a dough. The elasticity of the dough is developed by the ingredients being dragged around and bounced against the pan sides, but this actually heats up the dough quite a lot through the circular friction. Maybe that sudden increase in heat will excite the yeast, but an over-warm dough and a quick fermentation are not going to give you a great bread.

The proving function that kicks in after the kneading is also cause for concern, as overheating is common during that phase. The heating element at the bottom of the bread machine starts warming up to help the dough to prove, but this is all too quick and almost brutal – again, the dough being too warm during proving doesn't make a good bread. And to make matters worse, it seems that the bread is only rising once after the initial kneading, against the classic two rises that is usual in artisan baking, which deprives the loaf of the extra time it needs to develop a better taste and structure.

These are the main points of difference between artisan baking and bread machines – and they are quite fundamental differences. To bake bread well in a machine, you need to look at your bread maker from another angle, very much as a tool that requires your involvement and benefits from your acquired knowledge and your own experience. Don't simply chuck in all the ingredients and leave it to the machine, as its programmes are designed for a quick result and don't take into account the many factors that make a great loaf.

But enough of the negatives; in researching this book I definitely enjoyed working with my bread machines and I totally get why some people are so fond of them. We shouldn't be too judgemental over their use: they are convenient, less messy, and they might also be the first taste of baking for a lot of people, who might actually become inspired to move on to hand kneading and embracing the whole artisan baking 'way of life'.

The Fundamentals:
The Four Basic Ingredients

I t is important to quickly go over some technical knowledge behind baking before we get started on the recipes, as it will help you to avoid making frustrating mistakes along the way. Baking bread – whether by hand or using the bread machine – requires many steps, but even at its most basic level, there are four key ingredients that are vital for a good-quality loaf.

YEAST

Yeast has two important functions in bread making. First, it acts as a leavening agent to allow the bread to rise and create a more airy, lighter texture. Secondly, in conjunction with gluten, yeast adds strength to a dough. When it comes to using yeast, it is important to remember that in order for yeast to multiply, it needs warmth and sugar and hates direct contact with salt.

Yeast is a vital component of fermentation; most of the epic failures that we experience when starting our bread journey are linked to not being aware enough of the paramount importance of achieving and maintaining a healthy fermentation.

WHAT IS FERMENTATION?

We may think that since the machine is supposed to do everything for us, we don't have to bother too much about how bread works, but I would say very much the contrary: you need to understand the principles of fermentation if you want to master your bread machine in an artisan way. It is important to remember that there are three key temperatures involved in fermentation:

1) Fridge temperature, 4–5°C (40–41°F) – this is when your fermentation is dormant; not stopped altogether but slowly active, which is useful if you want to extend the proving of your doughs (cold proving) in order to develop more subtle flavours.

2) The perfect temperature – this is 24.6°C (76.2°F), and this is when fermentation and dough development are going to be at their best. It's a pretty precise measurement, but if you can keep your proving around that temperature no matter what the season and the air temperature, you will be more certain of obtaining a decent loaf.

3) Baking temperature – at 50°C (122°F) your yeast starts to be killed (this usually happens within 10 minutes of your bread being placed in the oven).

Consequently, there's a big difference when you're proving a dough at 15°C (59°F) and proving it at 24°C (75°F). At the other end of the temperature spectrum, if you're proving your dough at 40°C (104°F), this will be far too hot and far too quick (with a serious risk of over-proving) and won't give you a good fermentation or flavour.

Understanding the roles of these three different temperatures and their effects on your loaf will help you to avoid making a lot of the mistakes made by home bakers. I would even say that not observing temperature rules is the main pitfall in bread making – you must work with your environment!

In a nutshell, the yeast used in bread making is commonly called baker's yeast, which is a single-celled microorganism, a fungus of the species *Saccharomyces cerevisiae*, which is the same culture that's used in alcoholic fermentation in the brewing world.

Like any other living organism, yeast cells will multiply only if they are provided with food, water and a favourable environment. The food comes from the transformation of the starch in the flour through enzyme activity: starch forms a complex sugar, which the enzymes present in flour will break down into simple sugars that are directly accessible by the yeast, thus kick-starting the fermentation process. Water is already present in very minimal amounts in the flour, but this is mainly added in more significant quantities at the kneading stage. The environment is all about the temperature, and as mentioned above, this will increase or decrease the fermentation activity.

Food, water and temperature together provide yeast cells with the correct environment for them to start their work producing carbon dioxide and alcohol (ethanol), which leavens the dough (makes it rise) in the process. Fermentation brings carbon dioxide and aroma to the dough, and the carbon dioxide trapped in the gluten network gives the dough volume during proving.

As a baker, it is your role (and it is a learned skill!) to promote fermentation in a controlled manner, and even using a bread machine, you will still have to observe the same rules.

So, what sort of yeast should you use: fresh or dried? The bread machine recipe books I consulted seem to suggest the use of dried yeast exclusively; I tried both during my trials, but in reality, fresh yeast worked just as well. The only difference is that dried yeast is more convenient than fresh in a home setting, as it has a longer shelf life and it can be kept at room temperature, whereas fresh yeast needs to be stored in the fridge for a maximum of 2 weeks and can't be frozen (the freezing process will drastically interfere with the quality of your fermentation, if not kill it!).

We will be using dried yeast in this book for the reasons above. One thing to note if you want to use fresh is that dried yeast has a higher concentration of yeast per gram than fresh, so you will need less of it. The accepted convention is 50% less dried than fresh yeast, so if you've got a recipe using dried yeast but you're keen to use fresh, you'll have to double the quantity.

WATER

This is probably the ingredient that's most taken for granted when it comes to making bread, but actually it's a very important one because its role is to help the baker control the temperature of the bread and consequently achieve the best fermentation. The temperature of the water you use is more important than whether or not you should be using mineral water or tap water: tap water is the norm in bakeries (some bakers install a water-softener device in their premises, but as a home baker don't bother: your tap water will be fine!).

In an artisan bakery, the Head Baker will take the temperature of the mixing room and the flour before deciding what the temperature of the water should be for the mixing. Let's explain this more precisely: for example, it is a very hot summer's day, so the bakery will be even hotter because of the ovens being on, but the piled bags of flour will have also stored that excessive heat. So in that case, using warm water for preparing a batch of bread is going to have some serious consequences: a very warm dough will ferment far too quickly and be difficult to work with (over-proving will become a real threat). The baker therefore will have to lower the temperature of the water (possibly even use chilled water) to bring down the overall temperature of the dough to the perfect level (24–25°C/75–77°F). Obviously, in the winter this will be the total opposite: a cold bakery and a cold flour will require warm water to help raise the temperature of the dough. It's very much a balancing act!

Saying that, due to the way bread machines work, there is a natural tendency for the dough to get overheated during kneading because of the mechanical friction against the pan, so you may find it's better to use cooler water at all times.

FLOUR

In artisan baking, when we mention flour we think strong white flour – a flour with a higher gluten ratio than ordinary baking flours, at 12 to 13% – rather than plain flour, which contains less gluten, at 8 to 10%. Gluten is a protein that binds naturally, because as soon as the gluten molecules are in contact with a liquid they merge together, forming a tighter and tighter network over time, which will trap the fermentation first and later on the steam produced during baking. Kneading by hand, in a mixer or in the bread machine simply speeds up the natural binding of the gluten present in the flour. Gluten is definitely an ally you need in order to create a nice plump loaf.

The sky is your limit regarding the bread you could create from the many different types of flour available. Below is not a comprehensive guide to flour, just enough information for you to know the difference between them and what each type is best used for.

Strong and very strong white flour

For a good volume in your loaf it is important to use strong flour (French T55) or very strong flour (French T65), both of which have been milled from hard wheat and contain a higher ratio of gluten. European strong flour will be around 12 to 14% gluten; some American flour can be even stronger, with 15 or 16% gluten content; but Canadian wheat of the Manitoba type is very strong, at 18%, and is usually used for Viennoiserie. I would say that an excess of gluten is not necessarily the best option, but you do need a decent amount for successful bread making.

Plain flour

This is more of a cake and pastry flour. It is made from softer grains, which are planted later in the spring and haven't fully developed their gluten by harvest time. It is difficult to make bread with just plain flour, but if you wanted to do so in order to dilute a loaf's gluten content, you could mix some with very strong flour. I would advise a maximum ratio of 50:50 to ensure a good texture though, as too little gluten will reduce the volume of the bread.

Unbleached white flour

This is still a strong flour but it has not been interfered with by the bleaching treatment used by millers to improve the structuring capacity and to speed up the ageing process so the flour can be used more quickly. In an unbleached flour, the flour is left to age naturally, preserving many nutrients and also the natural pigmentation of the flour – hence its creamy, light-yellow tones. Definitely a flour worth considering if you want to make a healthy loaf.

Organic flour

Even if the recipes in this book don't involve the use of organic ingredients, going organic is very much part of the artisan approach. In order to be certified organic, a flour will have had to pass some specific standards for production that go all the way back to growing the crops. These must be grown pesticide-free, and chemical fertilisers are not allowed on organic fields, which is definitely a plus nowadays when people are questioning more and more where their food comes from. Any type of organic flour should be on your radar, but something to remember is that their consistency may vary a lot, which is why some professional bakers don't like to work with them. But in a domestic context, using organic flour with your bread machine will bring you the assurance that you're producing a healthy, nutritious and ethically sound loaf.

Wholemeal flour

In a wholemeal flour, the whole grain is used to make a more nutritious flour. To rewind back to white flour, basically, looking at a bag of white flour is like staring at a bag of sugar, as it is composed mainly of starch. In wholemeal flour, all the parts of the grain are used: bran, endosperm (which is the part of the grain that's kept in white flour and is full of starch) and wheatgerm, so consequently all of the goodness of the grain is retained. I would say that in any of your breads, try to incorporate an element of wholemeal flour (which could be other types of grain, such as wholemeal rye, spelt, Khorasan, buckwheat, etc.) to enhance the nutritional quality of your bread.

It can be a strong flour, but the presence of bran in a flour makes it coarser and doesn't facilitate as much gluten binding as in white flour. For that reason, be aware of 100% wholemeal bread, as this will be very dense and on the flatish side – after all, a good bread should be a nice eating experience too! For a lighter crumb, consider adding some white flour, even if it is a small amount – as little as 10% white flour added to your wholemeal flour, for instance, will make it less dense but still packed with fibre and general goodness.

Brown flour

This is made of equal parts strong white flour and wholewheat flour for a lighter loaf with some of the benefits of a wholemeal flour. You can buy it already blended or you can just make it yourself by mixing very strong white flour and wholemeal flour in a 50:50 ratio.

Granary malthouse flour

If you want a change from making wholemeal bread, you could use granary flour (also called granary malthouse flour or simply malthouse or malted flour). Basically, this is a white flour with small amounts of rye and barley flour added, and enriched with toasted flaked malted wheat. The malt content of that flour can give a slightly bigger volume to your loaf, as malt is a natural improver. It will also help to produce a nice dark-coloured crust with a pleasant, slightly bitter taste.

Rye flour

Rye grain definitely has an element of rusticity, as it's very much a wild, tenacious and hardy grass that needs very little maintenance – the original ancient grain par excellence. Before it was extensively modified with the help of science in modern times, originally wheat was a crop that thrived in milder to hot climates (so far, archaeological evidence seems to confirm the Middle East as the birthplace of wheat farming ever since the Neolithic Period). Rye, on the other hand, thrives in colder temperatures (it is the only crop that can germinate at freezing temperatures), so naturally it is the grain that's predominantly grown in Northern and Eastern Europe.

Rye grain produces a fantastic flour that's full of strong flavours and is naturally low in gluten, which is certainly of great interest for gluten-intolerant people. And being low in gluten (and a weak type of gluten, too) means that rye bread will always lack volume (a 100% rye bread will be very flat indeed!), so these loaves are better off being baked in a tin, which, of course, absolutely suits the bread machine process.

Ancient grains

Flours made from ancient grains are very interesting to use in baking, as they are highly nutritious and packed with a lot of subtle flavours. They are very high in gluten, but it is actually a very water-soluble gluten that's easily weakened during the baking process and therefore highly digestible. You could use them on their own or mix them with white flour, and like rye bread, they will give you a less stable dough, structurally speaking, than that for gluten-rich white breads.

Ancient grains regroup different varieties of primitive wheat, such as spelt, Khorasan (Kamut is often seen as another type of ancient grain but it is actually a brand name of Khorasan flour), emmer (sometimes called farro) and einkorn (probably the original wild wheat, this is a very rustic flour with a very coarse, granular aspect like semolina or cornmeal and is better mixed with other more refined flours).

Gluten-free flour

It's written on the can, it's missing a crucial component of traditional bread making, but it is worth saying that gluten-free flours can bring interesting flavours to your bread if mixed into your regular strong white flour (quinoa flour has a very strong, earthy flavour and needs to be used with parsimony). Obviously, you need to make sure that you only use a small amount in your mix as it could lead to lack of volume in your finished loaf, but in bread, what is big is not always the best!

SALT

Try to use natural fine sea salt as much as you can, which is easily obtainable, even in local supermarkets. There's nothing wrong with using table or cooking salt, but it contains a bit of chemistry with the addition of an anti-caking agent with a sinister-sounding name straight out of *Arsenic and Old Lace* called potassium ferrocyanide. It's probably very safe, but why not simply use natural, unadulterated salt in your baking instead?!

Salt plays three roles in bread:

1) Taste – the obvious one!

2) Control – there is a correlation between salt content and yeast activity: when yeast comes into direct contact with the salt, it will be cured through osmosis by the salt and killed after a very short while. Of course, when used in a dough, the two ingredients are partly separated by the flour and the water, but still, the yeast activity will be affected by the salt, so a baker will use the killing property of salt to extend the fermentation.

3) Structure – a lesser-known fact about salt is that it will react with the gluten contained in the flour and will harden it,

helping you to build your loaf. Forgetting to add salt to your dough will result not only in a very bland loaf but a very flat one too!

KNEADING, PROVING, SHAPING AND BAKING: THE DIFFERENCE BETWEEN BREAD MACHINE AND ARTISAN BAKING PROCESSES

When I started experimenting with my bread machines by just following the instruction booklet to make a basic loaf, I immediately noticed that the process was very different from what I am used to doing by hand, with the dough going through distinct operations during its journey. In a bread machine, the idea is for the dough to never leave the pan; so after kneading, the dough starts proving (in the FRENCH bake programme option, for instance, it is even kneaded again for a little while halfway through proving, then left to rise one more time), and at the end it is baked straight from that proving stage, with no shaping involved.

For an artisan baker, all this goes totally against what we have learned during our formative years! My dough-making by hand would go through many more stages, including typically:

1) Kneading – working the dough for 8 to 12 minutes.
2) First rise – sometimes called bulk rise or bulk fermentation, this process lasts around 1 hour 30 minutes when using baker's yeast, and 4 to 5 hours for a sourdough fermentation. This is when the fermentation and the dough development are going to be at their best.
3) Shaping – this is divided into three steps:
    a) Pre-shaping – giving a rough outline of the desired shape and further structuring the loaf.

b) Bench rest or intermediate proving – this is when the dough is left to recover from its handling by the baker and the gluten is allowed to relax before shaping. This takes 5 to 20 minutes maximum.

c) Final shaping – the last attempt at structuring your loaf by tightening up the gluten.

4) Second rise – this lasts 1 hour to 1 hour 30 minutes in normal yeasted dough and 2 to 3 hours for a sourdough loaf.

5) Baking – the baking time will vary according to the size and the weight of the loaf or the type of flour used.

So, back to the bread machine. Let's look at its first stage. The kneading is straightforward and uncomplicated: a mixing blade is locked at the bottom of the removal pan, and when all the ingredients are loaded into the pan, the blade drags those ingredients towards the bottom to be mixed. This differs from a classic freestanding mixer in that the kneading is initiated from the top by the hook, but this other approach works absolutely fine, too – you may need to scrape the sides and especially the corners where the flour can accumulate unmixed to make sure all the ingredients are well blended.

Proving is a crucial phase in fermentation, and in a bread machine, that stage is pretty much reduced to a standard time under a proving temperature, over which the home baker has no real control. It's usually quite warm in the machine, probably rushing fermentation, which can result in a noticeably weaker flavour in the final product.

Folding the dough during the middle of the first rise is not part of the bread machine process, and any shaping simply boils down to how the dough is left after kneading.

As for the baking, the bread seems always to be on the light colour side even if it is left on the EXTRA BAKE setting. I found it impossible to get a good crust with a strong caramelisation of the natural sugars at the top of the loaf that's so full of flavour and crunchy. This is because the absence of steam production in the bread machine during baking makes it hard for that dark outside to develop, especially on the top. It is also important to mention that not only do most bread machine recipes seem to rely on using sugar to activate the fermentation and give a bit more colour to the crumb, they also add fat for a softer crumb and to extend the shelf life of the loaf. Bread, in the eye of an artisan baker, should really be made from four key ingredients: water, flour, yeast and salt.

These are some of the fundamental differences between a bread maker and artisan baking. The aim of this book is to develop another way of looking at our machine by introducing a few traditional baking techniques alongside, and perhaps slowing down the machine process to be at a pace with the natural rhythm of real bread. So, let's now look at how you could apply the principles of good baking to your bread machine.

USING THE BREAD MACHINE LIKE AN ARTISAN BAKER

Firstly, an artisan baker will usually use some sort of pre-fermentation to increase the flavour of their bread, and secondly, they will try to delay the fermentation process of the final dough to further develop the flavour but also to improve the digestibility of the bread and to help it to keep a bit longer than if it was made with a straight dough (the direct method).

You can make a loaf of bread in an hour if you use the FAST BAKE setting, but this method relies on incorporating a lot of yeast and sugar to speed up the fermentation. In this process, your bread rises too quickly and does not build up any interesting flavours, so it will feel heavier on the stomach and dry out quicker, too. But if you use a pre-ferment, your yeast is already at work preparing the ground for the loaf to come, allowing you to significantly reduce the amount of yeast added to the final dough.

WHAT IS A PRE-FERMENTATION?

The role of a pre-fermentation is to bring more subtle flavours to your loaf without making it too acidic, as well as to improve both the elasticity and structural strength of the dough and naturally extend the freshness of the bread. Your pre-ferment is the starting block upon which you build a great-tasting loaf – for me, this is the baking equivalent of making a flavoursome stock before cooking a delicious homemade stew!

Classically, there are two types of pre-ferment:

1) The poolish method: This method was originally invented in Poland and was introduced in France during the second half of the nineteenth century, when a few Austrian bakers settled in Paris (bringing with them the ancestor of the croissant – the *kipferl* – at the same time!). A poolish is composed of an equal quantity of water and flour (100% hydration) with the addition of a minimal amount of yeast. Once fully mixed together, the batter-like mixture is left to ferment slowly at room temperature for 45 minutes to 1 hour, then is placed in the fridge to slow down the yeast activity for 12 to 18 hours, although it can be kept in the fridge for up to 48 hours. The dough is ready when the centre of the poolish is slightly

caving in, showing optimal fermentation. This method gives an almost sweet taste to the dough.

2) The fermented (or old) dough method: This method simply uses a piece of dough that has been made the day before and kept overnight in the fridge, which is added to the final dough at the kneading stage. A fermented dough is best used within 24 hours, otherwise it could get over-acidic and unusable. Like the poolish method, the fermented dough method adds more flavour to the bread, with a more acidic undertone, and helps with the dough's elasticity and development when shaped and baked. In bakeries, you simply reserve part of today's dough to prepare tomorrow's bread, in an ongoing process.

DELAYING FERMENTATION

In a professional bakery, the baker will make extensive use of refrigeration to delay fermentation. This is done in order to achieve a very flavoursome loaf: fermentation in a cold environment is dormant, not totally blocked but just slowly active, which allows the flavours of the dough to develop. You can allow the dough a longer prove at the first or second rise, or at both of them, making the whole proving process last from 12 to 48 hours in a professional bakery. However, in a domestic environment, 12 to 18 hours is sufficient to get a great result, because the dough doesn't always keep well in a domestic fridge for a very long time. This is because there's a risk of your fermentation losing momentum, as your fridge is not as efficient at keeping a constant low temperature as a professional one.

Most of the recipes in this book rely on the use of a pre-ferment and an extended prove to achieve a better-tasting bread.

AUTOLYSE

In combination with a long fermentation, the use of an autolyse method could improve your bread making. An autolyse allows a better stretch in the dough, even if it slightly decreases the volume of the loaf. How is this done? The salt is called a hydrophilic ingredient, which means that, in a mix, it will always divert some of the water towards itself without sharing it further.

When applying an autolyse method to your bread, you simply mix all of the water and flour that's listed in the recipe for a very short time (2 or 3 minutes) without adding the salt and yeast – you don't want the dough to start fermenting. The absence of salt in the dough allows the maximum absorption of the water by the flour, which makes the dough more elastic. An autolyse also facilitates the artificial and gradual destruction of the gluten, a reaction that is used at times by a baker to weaken an excessively strong flour. This technique is very efficient and must be limited to between 20 minutes and 1 hour 30 minutes maximum, because after that the gluten may be damaged irreversibly, turning your dough into a very soft, unusable mass. The rest of the ingredients (primarily salt and yeast) are added at the end of the resting time when kneading resumes, although the dough requires less kneading because the gluten will have started already to bind naturally by itself during that rest.

CHECKING THE GLUTEN DEVELOPMENT OF A DOUGH

To know if a bread has been sufficiently kneaded or not is important information for any baker, as it will determine if your loaf is going to have a good volume as well as a great general appearance. In a bakery, the baker in charge of mixing will stop the machine regularly to check if the gluten network of the dough is fully formed or not, as getting a good stretch on a dough is an indication of the quality of the batch in the making. A fully developed gluten network will trap the carbon dioxide originating in the bread during all the fermentation stages (first and second rises) as well as the steam produced during baking, which together increase the volume of the loaf.

This gluten network check is called the window pane test. It consists in taking a portion of dough and stretching it very delicately, working up and down and rotating it as if you are making a mini pizza, to the point that the dough has been turned into a near-transparent membrane. This is your wall of gluten that will trap the carbon dioxide and steam later on in the loaf's journey.

It's a very humble action, but baking is just a succession of such simple actions, and when these are knowledgeably put together, they make a great loaf!

EQUIPMENT

Before we get into the basic techniques, it's worth looking at what equipment you will need to create artisan breads by hand and with your bread machine.

Bread machines are usually presented as the only tool you need to make bread, but since I'm using my machine punctually rather than constantly from beginning to end, there are a few simple but essential bits of equipment you will need to accompany your home baking:

- A good-quality set of scales for accuracy. It's not only dry ingredients that you will be weighing, but also liquids, as the markings on the side of a jug are never 100% correct.
- Collection of different-sized mixing bowls. Always handy to have.
- Dough scraper. The Swiss Army knife of baking – you can cut and scrape dough with it, spread cream or jam, and even use it as a spatula to clean dough off surfaces. It is absolutely fundamental to making bread – a real must-have.
- A pastry brush for egg-washing or glazing loaves.
- A proving basket (round, long, or of both types!). Useful if you decide to bake your loaf in the oven rather than the bread machine and you want a different shape.
- Baking sheets, trays or a baking stone. These will help you to bake breads in proving baskets in the oven.
- Pizza peel. Allows a loaf to be cleanly lifted onto a baking stone or an upturned tray for an artisan finish.
- Baking tin. A large 900g (2lb) tin is always a good standard size.
- A small sharp knife or a packet of shaving razor blades. Useful for scoring bread.
- Shower caps are great for preventing your doughs from crusting during the proving phase, and are not single-use like cling film (beeswax is a very good eco-friendly alternative).
- Pen thermometer. This will help you to know the exact temperature in your kitchen and your dough at the end of kneading. A crucial bit of your baking paraphernalia!

- Water sprayer. You need steam for a good crust, and I found that spraying the inside of the bread machine or a baking tray at the bottom of the oven helps tremendously to obtain a decent colour on the top of your loaf (never dark enough for me, but I'm a well-done crust aficionado!).
- Rolling pin.
- Wire cooling racks.

BASIC TECHNIQUES: KNEADING AND SHAPING BY HAND

You may prefer to knead your bread by hand and then finish it in the bread machine, or you may want to knead your loaf in the machine then shape it by hand before putting it back into the pan for baking, or even bake it in the oven.

Kneading doesn't have to be a long, strenuous operation: you can get a perfectly developed dough by hand within 6 minutes of kneading – let's say 6 to 8 minutes is enough, perhaps 10 minutes maximum if your pace is a bit slower. Kneading for an extended amount of time is unnecessary and a waste of your energy – it may be useful to note that the risk of over-kneading is extremely unlikely when it's done by hand.

First of all, put your four basic ingredients – yeast, water, flour and salt – in the bowl and start combining them using a dough scraper. When the dough is just starting to come together, swap the scraper for your hand (and only one hand; if you're diving into your mix with both hands, you're in for a messy affair!) to mop up the remaining flour that is usually left at the bottom of the mixing bowl. Very importantly, clean the side of the bowl using the small rounded edge of your scraper. This is a worthwhile job as too much dough is usually left unused when it should be part of the loaf – the old-school adage of waste not want not applies here!

As soon as the dough comes together, turn it out onto a flourless worktop – the kneading is about to start. The reason you want to do this without a dusting of flour is simply to avoid unaccounted amounts of flour being incorporated into your dough, as this will radically change your recipe. In this situation, the scraper is really handy: scraping the dough at regular intervals during kneading will speed up the development of your dough without any extra flour being thrown in in random quantities.

When you have a roughly formed dough, start stretching it by digging the heel of the combining hand (the already sticky one!) right into the dough. The other hand (the clean, or cleanish, one) will be pinning down the budding loaf on one end to get a good stretch. Fold the dough back onto itself as if in a loop (alternatively, you could simply roll it back if that's easier for you), then start again; the dough will stick and, as mentioned above, then you can use the scraper to bring it back together and carry on with the process. With the other hand, push the dough sideways to make it rotate and repeat the action of stretch-fold (or roll), back-stretch, etc. Kneading must be done at a pretty active pace: if you go slowly, you will be bogged down in a very uncomfortable situation, resulting in dough all over your hands and the work surface.

When your dough starts to get smoother, you can switch to another way of kneading: folding the dough towards you and then pushing it away from you, rotating it each time. At this point it is no longer your arms doing the bulk of the work but the weight of your body, which makes this a much easier and less tiring method of kneading. You'll still have to use your scraper, though, in case the dough starts to stick to the worktop again.

When you have finished kneading, shape the loaf into a ball by rotating the dough on the same spot – its slight stickiness will help you to get the loaf rounder and rounder and firmer, too. Structuring the dough straight after the kneading like this increases the chances of better dough development as the loaf enters the proving stage.

SHAPING

As mentioned on page 16, shaping involves three distinct actions:
1) Pre-shaping.
2) Bench rest.
3) Final shaping.

These successive steps will help to improve the volume gained in the loaf during baking. The technique differs slightly depending on whether you are preparing a round or long loaf.

SHAPING A ROUND LOAF

After the bench rest, place the loosely rounded piece of dough right in front of you; the top of the rested bread should be smooth and underneath wrinkly (this is called the seam). Turn the dough over and start firmly folding the sides of the loaf into the middle of the dough, going around it once. Turn it over again so the smooth side is up and the seam is down, place both hands on the sides of the loaf and start rotating it on the same spot (don't start travelling all over the place!) until the whole loaf feels tighter. Don't overdo it, otherwise you will end up with the loaf inside out! You're looking to achieve tension and structure.

Again, don't use any additional flour during shaping – or if it's really sticky and you absolutely must, use as little as possible. Dry flour on the outside of the loaf prevents a tight shaping and interferes with the sealing of the loaf.

Once you have shaped the loaf, place it upside down (smooth side down/seam up) in a heavily floured basket and cover with a plastic sheet or plastic bag to avoid crusting. If you're using the pan of the bread machine, add the shaped loaf to it seam side down with the smooth top facing up.

SHAPING A LONG LOAF

Obviously, this is a shape that's not compatible with the pan of your bread machine, so baking must be done in the oven!

Just as you did for the round loaf, make sure the dough is placed right in front of you. This time, turn it over with the wrinkly seam facing up. Gently flatten the elongated piece of dough and fold it once towards you to form a fat sausage. Seal the fold with the heel of your hand, then fold it again so that your loaf looks rounder and fatter. At that point, turn it over with the smooth part facing upwards and the line (the seam) created through the two consecutive foldings set against the worktop. Rock the loaf back and forth with some pressure to make it tight.

Your loaf is now ready, so place it upside down in an oblong floured proving basket and cover with a clean tea towel or similar.

Round or long, the loaf will now continue its fermentation journey with the second rise.

SCORING THE BREAD

Most loaves are scored on top with a sharp knife to create various attractive patterns so that they will catch the eye of potential customers, but the cuts on bread are also there for a practical reason: to help with the loaf development and general appearance. These cuts create exit vents for the steam produced during baking and stops it bursting the bread crust in an unsightly manner.

For scoring bread, the best tool is a razor blade – the blade of a knife is far too thick to make a neat incision, and could actually deflate your loaf, ruining it at the last second after many hours of dedicated work! To use a razor blade efficiently, you only need to cut the loaf with a corner of the blade – not the whole edge, as this would plough into the dough rather than cutting it neatly, which again runs the danger of destroying the bread.

In bread machines, the loaves are rarely scored, it seems, but nothing prevents you from doing so. If you are using your oven for the baking stage instead of the bread machine, and you proved your bread in a basket, scoring will help you to get a good result. So have a go, practise your scoring skills!

ALTERNATIVE APPROACHES WHEN USING THE BREAD MACHINE

The way we're going to use our bread machine will have to take all of those factors mentioned above into account, meaning that to get a really good loaf, the dough will certainly not stay in the bread pan from start to finish.

Generally speaking, we want to look at bread machines from another angle; yes, it's a machine that does the job for us, but it's also a machine that should work a bit more in partnership with us, with more involvement from us without being too taxing time-wise. It takes just a few adjustments to make use of the bread machine and get it more in tune with real bread making.

What we propose is to make suggestions on how to use the bread machine in a more hands-on way. The following options could be applied to any of the recipes given in the book – each are followed by a short description to illustrate what they mean concretely:

OPTION 1:

- Pre-fermentation
- Kneading in the bread machine
- First rise/bulk fermentation in the bread machine
- Shaping out of the bread machine
- Second rise in the bread machine
- Baking in the bread machine

In this option, the home baker has to assess the temperature of the dough: if it's too warm as a consequence of the kneading programme, switch off the machine with the dough left in the pan in the bread machine with the lid shut. If the dough feels cold, it could benefit from starting the programmed proving temperature automatically just after the kneading is finished. If so, switch off the machine after a while so the dough can rise more naturally without being subjected to unnecessary prolonged heat. Spraying the inside of the bread machine with water will help to add necessary moisture during the proving.

After proving, take the dough out of the pan, lightly shape it and leave it, covered, on a clean surface for the bench rest (5 to 20 minutes maximum). The mixing blade should be removed from the pan or from the dough if the blade was stuck in it when it was taken out of the pan.

Bench rest over, give the dough its final shape and return it to the pan and place this in the bread machine. In preparation for this second rise, start the DOUGH programme again so the heated proving phase can be used straight after the dough gets its final shape. Again, spray the inside of the bread machine to add moisture during proving.

After the second rise, take the pan out of the bread machine and turn on the BAKE programme. Preheat the machine for 10 minutes then lock the pan back into place. Generously spray the inside of the bread machine with water and bake to the end of the baking cycle. After that, start a second BAKE programme to take the baking time to 1 hour 30 minutes in total.

OPTION 2

- Pre-fermentation
- Kneading in the bread machine
- First rise in the bread machine
- Shaping out of the bread machine
- Second rise out of the bread machine
- Baking in the oven

Once more, in this option the home baker has to assess the temperature of the dough as in Option 1.

After proving, take the dough out of the pan, lightly shape it and leave it to rise, covered loosely with cling film, a plastic bag or a shower cap, at room temperature for 30 to 45 minutes.

Then place it, still covered, in the fridge for 8 to 18 hours before baking.

Ahead of baking, take the loaf out of the fridge and leave it on the side, still covered, until the dough comes back to room temperature – 2 to 3 hours according to how much the loaf has been rising in the fridge and how warm your kitchen is.

For this option, the baking is done in the oven rather than the bread machine, in order to achieve a better caramelisation of the crust. Preheat the oven to 250°C, 230°C fan, gas mark 9 with a baking tray in the base of the oven. Spray the baking tray with water when you add the loaf, then bake for 30 to 35 minutes.

OPTION 3

- Pre-fermentation
- Kneading out of the bread machine
- First rise in the bread machine
- Shaping out of the bread machine
- Second rise out of the bread machine
- Baking in the oven

For this option, kneading is done by hand, not by the bread machine, on a smooth worktop, following the instructions on page 24.

Place the kneaded dough into the bread machine – with the proving function already on if the kitchen and the dough feel cold. Spray the inside of the bread machine with water before closing the lid.

After proving, take the dough out of the pan, lightly shape it and leave it, covered, on a clean surface for the bench rest (5 to 20 minutes maximum).

Bench rest over, give the dough its final shape, place it in a proving basket and return it to the pan, then cover the shaped loaf loosely with cling film, a plastic bag or a shower cap. Leave to rise at room temperature for 30 to 45 minutes. Then place it, still covered, in the fridge for 8 to 18 hours before baking.

Ahead of baking, take the loaf out of the fridge and leave it on the side, still covered, until the dough comes back to room temperature – 2 to 3 hours according to how much the loaf has been rising in the fridge and how warm your kitchen is.

For this option, the baking is done in the oven rather than the bread machine, in order to achieve a better caramelisation of the crust. Preheat the oven to 250°C, 230°C fan, gas mark 9 with a baking tray in the base of the oven. Spray the baking tray with water when you add the loaf, then bake for 30 to 35 minutes.

OPTION 4

- Pre-fermentation
- Kneading out of the bread machine
- First rise out of the bread machine
- Shaping out of the bread machine
- Second rise in the bread machine
- Baking in the bread machine

For this option, the kneading is done by hand, not by the bread machine, on a smooth worktop, following the instructions on page 24.

After kneading, cover the dough loosely with cling film, a plastic bag or a shower cap. Leave to rise at room temperature for 30 to 45 minutes. Then place it, still covered, in the fridge for 8 to 18 hours before baking.

Ahead of baking, take the loaf out of the fridge and leave it on the side, still covered, until the dough comes back to room temperature – 2 to 3 hours according to how much the loaf has been rising in the fridge and how warm your kitchen is.

Bench rest over, give the dough its final shape and return it to the pan and place it in the bread machine in preparation for the second rise.

After the second rise, take the pan out of the bread machine and turn on the BAKE programme. Preheat the machine for 10 minutes then lock the pan back into place. Generously spray the inside of the bread machine with water and bake to the end of the baking cycle. After that, start a second BAKE programme to take the baking time to 1 hour 30 minutes in total.

OPTION 5

- Pre-fermentation
- Kneading out of or in the bread machine
- First rise out of the bread machine
- Shaping out of the bread machine
- Second rise out of the bread machine
- Baking in or out of the bread machine

In this option, the two rises are extended through a cold fermentation that takes place over 3 days in the fridge. This method is for home bakers who are interested in increasing the flavour of their loaves. Of course, with extra long fermentations there is always a possibility for the loaf to over-ferment, but I'd say it's worth the risk for an improved flavour.

Here, you have several options, according to what you want to achieve and if you want a bit more control. The method allows you to take over the bread machine and also involve your hands for kneading, shaping or finishing the baking in the oven.

Knead the dough either by hand on a smooth worktop following the instructions on page 24, or in the bread machine.

After kneading, cover the dough loosely with cling film, a plastic bag or a shower cap. Leave to rise at room temperature for 30 to 45 minutes. Then place it, still covered, in the fridge for 8 to 18 hours before baking.

Take the loaf out of the fridge and leave it on the side, still covered, until the dough comes back to room temperature – 2 to 3 hours according to how much the loaf has been rising in the fridge and how warm your kitchen is.

Bench rest over, give the dough its final shape and cover the dough loosely with cling film, a plastic bag or a shower cap. Leave to rise at room temperature for 30 to 45 minutes. Then place it, still covered, in the fridge for 8 to 18 hours for a second rise.

After the second rise, if you are using the bread machine, turn on the BAKE programme. Preheat the machine for 10 minutes then lock the pan back into place (by doing so, the dough is subjected immediately to the heat as if it was baked in the usual way in an oven). Generously spray the inside of the bread machine with water and bake to the end of the baking cycle. After that, start a second BAKE programme to take the baking time to 1 hour 30 minutes in total. If you want to bake in the oven, preheat the oven to 250°C, 230°C fan, gas mark 9 with a baking tray in the base of the oven. Spray the baking tray with water when you add the loaf, then bake for 30 to 35 minutes.

WHICH PROGRAMMES TO USE IN YOUR BREAD MACHINE?

With a bread machine you've usually got a choice of 12 different programmes that are very similarly named from one manufacturer to another:

1) BASIC
2) FRENCH
3) WHOLEMEAL
4) QUICK
5) SWEET
6) FAST I
7) FAST II
8) DOUGH
9) GLUTEN-FREE
10) CAKE
11) SANDWICH
12) BAKE

Some bread machines may replace one programme with another one, such as a jam-making cycle, but they all offer a similar range of options.

During my experiments, I actually used very few of the programmes; the two main ones were the BAKE and DOUGH programmes, and occasionally FRENCH and WHOLEMEAL, as those cycles tend to be longer and I wanted to test them to see what they produced. I wasn't interested in the FAST or

SUPERFAST settings; they're designed to make quick breads and so rely on a higher level of yeast and sugar, which doesn't appeal to me at all. The speedy hot bread produced at the end of those cycles may be a reward, but even an awful bread always tastes nice when hot!

So, by sticking principally to the BAKE and DOUGH cycles, I found I had more control in the process: I could stop the kneading whenever I wanted, I could play with the proving phase the way I felt was best for my doughs, and as for the baking, again, I had more control on the length and level of caramelisation of the crust. I always prefer a final bake in the oven for a better colour.

The Recipes

Before we start, in the recipes in this book I'm applying a simple timeline with no cold proving involved. The reason behind this choice is not to over-complicate the methods by describing all the different options for each single recipe that are given on pages 39–153.

As mentioned earlier, in these recipes I've listed dried yeast in the ingredients. Where a pinch of yeast is specified, I appreciate that this is not exactly a precise measurement, but your scales won't be able to register the minute amount of yeast needed. Sprinkling a little yeast over the water and dissolving it will be more than enough to kick-start the fermentation. Where a weight is specified, small amounts are not always acknowledged by scales, so always go for a higher amount then go down to the desired amount – much easier!

BASIC WHITE LOAF

When I'm talking about a white loaf, I never really mean that it should be purely white. As I've said before, white bread is not the most nutritious loaf around, so I will always include an element of wholemeal flour in the mix to make it a bit healthier or at least bring out some flavour from the wholemeal flours. Wholemeal wheat, spelt, rye, ancient grains or even gluten-free flours all have distinct and interesting flavours: in the south-west of France, artisan bakers use Farine de Gaude, which is made out of roasted and ground corn kernels and gives a nice, slightly caramelised flavour to their loaves.

I will give different pre-fermentations here for this recipe, so you can test them out and see which you prefer or which is the most convenient for you to use. Like any pre-ferment, the poolish method will help you to cut down drastically on the amount of yeast added to the final dough (see Day 2), preventing your bread becoming stale quickly. This was one of my main concerns when I started researching this book, as a lot of the recipes relied on a high level of yeast for a quick rise, and a higher quantity of yeast makes the bread heavier on the stomach and less digestible, with less-interesting aromas.

POOLISH METHOD

DAY 1
100g (3½oz) water
100g (3½oz) strong white flour
Pinch of dried yeast

Combine all the poolish ingredients together in a mixing bowl, cover, and leave to ferment at room temperature for a couple of hours, then place in the fridge for anything from 12 to 48 hours.

DAY 2
Poolish from Day 1
2g (⅒oz) dried yeast
325g (11½oz) water
500g (1lb 2oz) strong white flour, plus extra for dusting
50g (1¾oz) wholemeal flour of your choice
11g (⅖oz) salt

On Day 2, take the poolish out of the fridge a couple of hours before you want to make your bread to allow it to reach room temperature.

In a bowl on a set of scales, start weighing the yeast, then weigh out the water into the pan. Remember the importance of the temperature of the water if you're kneading outside the bread machine. Dissolve the yeast in the water. Add the Day 1 poolish to the water and use some of the water to clean the poolish container so you're making the most of that long, flavoursome fermentation.

Weigh out the flours straight on top of the water and poolish. Measure the salt separately for accuracy's sake and place it on top of the flours. Start the DOUGH programme on your bread machine – the kneading time in a machine is usually quite long, at 10–20 minutes, with more kneading involved after a resting period. I would say that whatever the kneading method you choose, it should be done and dusted in about 6–8 minutes: kneading for longer won't necessarily give you a better dough development.

Stop the programme after that time, remove the dough, restart the DOUGH programme and return the dough to the pan when the kneading section is over and it is entering proving mode. The heating element for proving in a bread machine is firmly on the hot side and impossible to regulate, so the dough can warm up too quickly and interfere with the quality of the end product. If using the machine for proving, regularly check your dough and switch off the machine if you want to prove the loaf for longer. Alternatively, leave the dough to prove, covered, at room temperature. Either way, proving should normally take between 1 hour and 1 hour 30 minutes.

If you are shaping by hand, transfer the dough to a lightly floured work surface, then go around the dough

folding the corners in towards the middle, and turn it over. Cover the dough and give it a bench rest of 10–15 minutes.

After the bench rest is done, turn the dough over on a work surface without flour and fold it tightly towards the centre, going around the dough once. Turn over the dough so the smooth side is up, then place both hands on the side of the loaf and keep rotating it on the same spot until you feel the dough firming up and getting taller.

Place the shaped loaf in the bread machine pan or a proving basket, if you've got one. Let it prove for 1 hour to 1 hour 30 minutes, or until it has doubled in size.

Once you're ready to bake the bread, start the BAKE programme without the dough in the machine to preheat – about 10 minutes. Lock the pan into the bread machine, spray the inside of the machine with water and bake for 1 hour (you will have to start another BAKE programme to compensate for the preheating time). You might have to carry on with the baking for another 30 minutes to get a little bit more colour on the top of your loaf. Alternatively, use your oven for baking. You can use the bread machine pan in the oven safely, or transfer your loaf to a baking stone or put it on a tray in a hot oven preheated to 250°C, 230°C fan, gas mark 9 with a baking tray in the base of the oven. Spray the baking tray with water when you add the loaf, then bake for 30 minutes, or 40 minutes if you want a nice dark crust.

Remove the baked bread from the oven, leave to cool down for 5 minutes, then carefully take it out of the pan and transfer to a cooling rack. Enjoy still warm or leave it to cool right down before eating.

FERMENTED DOUGH METHOD

DAY 1
100g (3½oz) strong white flour
60g (2oz) water
Pinch of dried yeast

Combine all the Day 1 ingredients in a small bowl and mix to a rough dough. Transfer to a flourless work surface and mix quickly into a smooth dough – 2–3 minutes is more than enough. Place back in the bowl, cover with cling film, a shower cap, beeswax or a plastic bag and leave to prove at room temperature for 1 hour. Then place it, still covered, in the fridge for 8 to 18 hours before baking – maximum 24 hours.

DAY 2
160g (5½oz) fermented dough
325g (11½oz) water
2g (⅒oz) dried yeast
500g (1lb 2oz) strong white flour, plus extra for dusting
50g (1¾oz) wholemeal flour of your choice
11g (⅖oz) salt

On Day 2, take the fermented dough out of the fridge a couple of hours before you want to make your bread to allow it to reach room temperature.

Weigh out the water. Remember the importance of the temperature of the water if you're kneading outside the bread machine. Dissolve the yeast in the water. Add the fermented dough to the water.

Weigh out the flours straight on top of the water and dough. Make sure you measure the salt separately for accuracy's sake and place it on top of the flours. Start the DOUGH programme on your bread machine – the kneading time in a bread machine is usually quite long, at 10–20 minutes, with more kneading involved after a resting period. I would say that whatever the kneading method you choose, it should be done and dusted in about 6–8 minutes: kneading for longer won't necessarily give you a better dough development.

Stop the programme after that time, remove the dough, restart the DOUGH programme and return the dough to the pan when the kneading section of the programme is over and it is entering proving mode. If using the machine for proving, regularly check your dough and switch off the machine if you want to prove the loaf for longer. Alternatively, leave the dough to prove, covered, at room temperature. Either way, proving should normally take between 1 hour and 1 hour 30 minutes.

If you are shaping the dough by hand, transfer it to a lightly floured work surface, then go around the dough folding the corners in towards the middle, and turn it over. Cover the dough and give it a bench rest of 10–15 minutes.

After the bench rest is done, turn the dough over on a work surface without flour and fold it tightly towards the centre, going around the dough once. Turn over the dough so the smooth side is up, then place both hands on the side of the loaf and keep rotating it on the same spot until you feel the dough firming up and getting taller.

Place the shaped loaf in the bread machine pan or a proving basket, if you've got one. Let it prove for 1 hour to 1 hour 30 minutes, or until it has doubled in size.

Once you're ready to bake the bread, start the BAKE programme without the bread in the machine, to preheat – about 10 minutes. Lock the pan into the bread machine, spray the inside of the machine with the water sprayer and bake for 1 hour (you will have to start another BAKE programme to compensate for the preheating time). You might have to carry on with the baking for another 30 minutes to get a little bit more colour on the top of your loaf. Alternatively, use your oven for baking. You can use the bread machine pan in the oven safely, or transfer your loaf to a baking stone or put it on a tray in a hot oven preheated to 250°C, 230°C fan, gas mark 9 with a baking tray in the base of the oven. Spray the baking tray with water when you add the loaf, then bake for 30 minutes, or 40 minutes if you want a nice dark crust.

Remove the baked bread from the oven, leave to cool down for 5 minutes, then carefully take it out of the pan and transfer to a cooling rack. Enjoy still warm or leave it to cool right down before eating.

BROWN BREAD

Brown bread usually recommends a 50:50 combination of white and wholemeal flour for a lighter loaf, as a 100% wholemeal loaf will be very dense and heavy. I think it is good to welcome a little bit of lightness into our daily bread – and this is still a very nutritious and wholesome loaf. There's a recipe for a 70% wholemeal bread on page 59 just in case you're after a higher fibre content. Both recipes can be made using either a poolish method or a fermented dough method.

POOLISH METHOD

DAY 1
100g (3½oz) water
100g (3½oz) strong white flour
Pinch of dried yeast

Combine all the poolish ingredients together fully in a mixing bowl, cover, and leave to ferment at room temperature for a couple of hours, then place in the fridge for anything from 12 to 48 hours.

DAY 2
Poolish from Day 1
4g (⅛oz) dried yeast
270g (9½oz) water
225g (8oz) strong white flour, plus extra for dusting
225g (8oz) strong wholemeal flour of your choice
10g (⅓oz) salt

On Day 2, take the poolish out of the fridge a couple of hours before you want to make your bread to allow it to reach room temperature.

In a bowl on a set of scales, start weighing the yeast, then weigh out the water. Remember the importance of the temperature of the water if you're kneading outside the bread machine.

Weigh out the flours straight on top of the water and poolish. Make sure you measure the salt separately for accuracy's sake and place it on top of the flours. Start the DOUGH programme on your bread machine – the kneading time in a bread machine is usually quite long, at 10–20 minutes, with more kneading involved after a resting period. I would say that whatever the kneading method you choose, it should be done and dusted in about 6–8 minutes: kneading for longer won't necessarily give you a better dough development.

Stop the programme after that time, remove the dough, restart the DOUGH programme and return the dough to the pan when the kneading section of the programme is over and it is entering proving mode. If using the machine for proving, regularly check your dough and switch off the machine if you want to prove the loaf for longer. Alternatively, leave the dough to prove, covered, at room temperature. Either way, proving should normally take between 1 hour and 1 hour 30 minutes.

If you are shaping by hand, transfer the dough to a lightly floured work surface, then go around the dough folding the corners in towards the middle, and turn it over. Cover the dough and give it a bench rest of 10–15 minutes.

After the bench rest is done, turn the dough over on a work surface without flour and fold it tightly towards the centre, going around the dough once. Turn over the dough so the smooth side is up, then place both hands on the side of the loaf and keep rotating it on the same spot until you feel the dough firming up and getting taller.

Place the shaped loaf in the bread machine pan or a proving basket, if you've got one. Let it prove for 1 hour to 1 hour 30 minutes, or until it has doubled in size.

Once you're ready to bake the bread, start the BAKE programme without the bread in the machine, to preheat – about 10 minutes. Lock the pan into the bread machine, spray the inside of the machine with water and bake for 1 hour (you will have to start another BAKE programme to compensate for the preheating time). You might have to carry on with the baking for another 30 minutes to get a little bit more colour on the top of your loaf. Alternatively, use your oven for baking.

You can use the bread machine pan in the oven safely, or transfer your loaf to a baking stone or put it on a tray in a hot oven preheated to 250°C, 230°C fan, gas mark 9. Add another baking tray to the base of the oven. Spray the spare baking tray with water when you add the loaf, then bake for 30 minutes, or 40 minutes if you want a nice dark crust.

Remove the baked bread from the oven, leave to cool down for 5 minutes, then carefully take it out of the pan and transfer to a cooling rack. Enjoy still warm or leave it to cool right down before eating.

FERMENTED DOUGH METHOD

DAY 1
100g (3½oz) strong white flour
60g (2oz) water
Pinch of dried yeast

Combine all the Day 1 ingredients in a small bowl to a rough dough. Transfer to a flourless work surface and mix quickly into a smooth dough – 2–3 minutes is more than enough. Place back in the bowl, cover with cling film, a shower cap, beeswax or a plastic bag and leave to prove at room temperature for 1 hour. Then place it, still covered, in the fridge for 8 to 18 hours before baking – maximum 24 hours.

DAY 2
160g (5½oz) fermented dough
4g (⅛oz) dried yeast
310g (11oz) water
225g (8oz) strong white flour, plus extra for dusting
225g (8oz) strong wholemeal flour of your choice
9g (⅜oz) salt

On Day 2, take the fermented dough out of the fridge a couple of hours before you want to make your bread to allow it to reach room temperature.

In a bowl on a set of scales, start weighing the yeast, then weigh out the water. Remember the importance of the temperature of the water if you're kneading outside the bread machine. Dissolve the yeast in the water. Add the fermented dough to the water and use some of the water to clean the container so you're making the most of that flavoursome fermentation.

Weigh out the flours straight on top of the water and old dough. Make sure you measure the salt separately for accuracy's sake and place it on top of the flours. Start the DOUGH programme on your bread machine – the kneading time in a bread machine is usually quite long, at 10–20 minutes, with more kneading involved after a resting period. I would say that whatever the kneading method you choose, it should be done and dusted in about 6–8 minutes: kneading for longer won't necessarily give you a better dough development.

Stop the programme after that time, remove the dough, restart the DOUGH programme and return the dough to the pan when the kneading section of the programme is over and it is entering proving mode. If using the machine for proving, regularly check your dough and switch off the machine if you want to prove the loaf for longer. Alternatively, leave the dough to prove, covered, at room temperature. Either way, proving should normally take between 1 hour and 1 hour 30 minutes.

If you are shaping by hand, transfer the dough to a lightly floured work surface, then go around the dough folding the corners in towards the middle, and turn it over. Cover the dough and give it a bench rest of 10–15 minutes.

After the bench rest is done, turn the dough over on a work surface with no flour and fold it tightly towards the centre, going around the dough once. Turn over the dough so the smooth side is up, then place both hands on the side of the loaf and keep rotating it on the same spot until you feel the dough firming up and getting taller.

Place the shaped loaf in the bread machine pan or a proving basket, if you've got one. Let it prove for 1 hour to 1 hour 30 minutes, or until it has doubled in size.

Once you're ready to bake the bread, start the BAKE programme without the bread in the machine, to preheat – about 10 minutes. Lock the pan into the bread machine, spray the inside of the machine with water and bake for 1 hour (you will have to start another BAKE programme to compensate for the preheating time). You might have to carry on with the baking for another 30 minutes to get a little bit more colour on the top of your loaf. Alternatively, use your oven for baking. You can use the bread machine pan in the oven safely, or transfer your loaf to a baking stone or put it on a tray in a hot oven preheated to 250°C, 230°C fan, gas mark

9. Add another baking tray to the base of the oven. Spray the spare baking tray with water when you add the loaf, then bake for 30 minutes, or 40 minutes if you want a nice dark crust.

Remove the baked bread from the oven, leave to cool down for 5 minutes, then carefully take it out of the pan and transfer to a cooling rack. Enjoy still warm or leave it to cool right down before eating.

70% WHOLEMEAL LOAF

This is the more wholemeal version of the brown bread: it will be denser, but it answers the need for some of us for a higher fibre content and slow sugar release in our bread.

POOLISH METHOD

DAY 1
100g (3½oz) strong wholemeal flour
100g (3½oz) water
Pinch of dried yeast

Combine all the poolish ingredients together fully in a mixing bowl – it will turn into a thick mixture because of the bran contained in the wholemeal flour. Cover and leave to ferment at room temperature for a couple of hours, then place in the fridge for anything from 12 to 48 hours.

DAY 2
Poolish from Day 1
6g (⅕oz) dried yeast
300g (10½oz) water
130g (4⅗oz) strong white flour
320g (11⅓oz) strong wholemeal flour
9g (³⁄₁₀oz) natural fine salt

On Day 2, take the poolish out of the fridge a couple of hours before you want to make your bread to allow it to reach room temperature.

In a bowl on a set of scales, start weighing the yeast, then weigh out the water. Remember the importance of the temperature of the water if you're kneading outside the bread machine. Dissolve the yeast in the water. Add the Day 1 poolish to the water and use some of the water to clean the poolish container so you're making the most of that flavoursome fermentation.

Weigh out the flours straight on top of the water and poolish. Make sure you measure the salt separately for accuracy's sake and place it on top of the flours. Start the DOUGH programme on your bread machine – the kneading time in a bread machine is usually quite long, at 10–20 minutes, with more kneading involved after a resting period. I would say that whatever the kneading method you choose, it should be done and dusted in about 6–8 minutes: kneading for longer won't necessarily give you a better dough development.

Stop the programme after that time, remove the dough, restart the DOUGH programme and return the dough to the pan when the kneading section of the programme is over and it is entering proving mode. If using the machine for proving, regularly check your dough and switch off the machine if you want to prove the loaf for longer. Alternatively, leave the dough to prove, covered, at room temperature. Either way, proving should normally take between 1 hour and 1 hour 30 minutes.

If you are shaping by hand, transfer the dough to a lightly floured work surface, then go around the dough

folding the corners in towards the middle, and turn it over. Cover the dough and give it a bench rest of 10–15 minutes.

After the bench rest is done, turn the dough over on a work surface without flour and fold it tightly towards the centre, going around the dough once. Turn over the dough so the smooth side is up, then place both hands on the side of the loaf and keep rotating it on the same spot until you feel the dough firming up and getting taller.

Place the shaped loaf in the bread machine pan or a proving basket, if you've got one. Let it prove for 1 hour to 1 hour 30 minutes, or until it has doubled in size.

Once you're ready to bake the bread, start the BAKE programme without the bread in the machine, to preheat – about 10 minutes. Lock the pan into the bread machine, spray the inside of the machine with water and bake for 1 hour (you will have to start another BAKE programme to compensate for the preheating time). You might have to carry on with the baking for another 30 minutes to get a little bit more colour on the top of your loaf. Alternatively, use your oven for baking. You can use the bread machine pan in the oven safely, or transfer your loaf to a baking stone or put it on a tray in a hot oven preheated to 250°C, 230°C fan, gas mark 9. Place another baking tray in the base of the oven.

Spray the spare baking tray with water when you add the loaf, then bake for 30 minutes, or 40 minutes if you want a nice dark crust.

Remove the baked bread from the oven, leave to cool down for 5 minutes, then carefully take it out of the pan and transfer to a cooling rack. Enjoy still warm or leave it to cool right down before eating.

FERMENTED DOUGH METHOD

DAY 1
100g (3½oz) strong white flour
60g (2oz) water
Pinch of dried yeast

Combine all the ingredients in a small bowl to a rough dough. Transfer to a flourless work surface and mix quickly into a smooth dough – 2–3 minutes is more than enough. Place back in the bowl, cover with cling film, a shower cap, beeswax or a plastic bag and leave to prove at room temperature for 1 hour. Then place it, still covered, in the fridge for 8 to 18 hours before baking – maximum 24 hours.

DAY 2
160g (5½oz) fermented dough
6g (⅕oz)dried yeast
340g (12oz) water
30g (1oz) strong white flour, plus extra for dusting
420g (14⅘oz) strong wholemeal flour of your choice
9g (⅗oz) salt

On Day 2, take the fermented dough out of the fridge a couple of hours before you want to make your bread to allow it to reach room temperature.

In a bowl on a set of scales, start weighing the yeast, then weigh out the water. Remember the importance of the temperature of the water if you're kneading outside the bread machine. Dissolve the yeast in the water. Add the fermented dough to the water.

Weigh out the flours straight on top of the water and the fermented dough. Make sure you measure the salt separately for accuracy's sake and place it on top of the flours. Start the DOUGH programme on your bread machine – the kneading time in a bread machine is usually quite long, at 10–20 minutes, with more kneading involved after a resting period. I would say that whatever the kneading method you choose, it should be done and dusted in about 6–8 minutes: kneading for longer won't necessarily give you a better dough development.

Stop the programme after that time, remove the dough, restart the DOUGH programme and return the dough to the pan when the kneading section of the programme is over and it is entering proving mode. If using the machine for proving, regularly check your dough and switch off the machine if you want to prove the loaf for longer. Alternatively, leave the dough to prove, covered, at room temperature. Either way, proving should normally take between 1 hour and 1 hour 30 minutes.

If you are shaping by hand, transfer the dough to a lightly floured work surface, then go around the dough folding the corners in towards the middle, and turn it over. Cover the dough and give it a bench rest of 10–15 minutes.

After the bench rest is done, turn the dough over on a work surface without flour and fold it tightly towards the centre, going around the dough once. Turn over the dough so the smooth side is up, then place both hands on the side of the loaf and keep rotating it on the same spot until you feel the dough firming up and getting taller.

Place the shaped loaf in the bread machine pan or a proving basket, if you've got one. Let it prove for 1 hour to 1 hour 30 minutes, or until it has doubled in size.

Once you're ready to bake the bread, start the BAKE programme without the bread in the machine, to preheat – about 10 minutes. Lock the pan into the bread machine, spray the inside of the machine with water and bake for 1 hour (you will have to start another BAKE programme to compensate for the preheating time). You might have to carry on with the baking for another 30 minutes to get a little bit more colour on the top of your loaf. Alternatively, use your oven for baking. You can use the bread machine pan in the oven safely, or transfer your loaf to a baking stone or put it on a tray in a hot oven preheated to 250°C, 230°C fan, gas mark 9. Place another baking tray in the base of the oven. Spray the spare baking tray with water when you add

the loaf, then bake for 30 minutes, or 40 minutes if you want a nice dark crust.

Remove the baked bread from the oven, leave to cool down for 5 minutes, then carefully take it out of the pan and transfer to a cooling rack. Enjoy still warm or leave it to cool right down before eating.

GRANARY BREAD

A granary bread always gives a nice textured loaf with large pieces of malted rolled wheat, and in this recipe, seeds are added for good measure and wholesomeness.

POOLISH METHOD

DAY 1
100g (3½oz) wholemeal spelt
100g (3½oz) water
Pinch of yeast

Combine all the poolish ingredients together fully in a mixing bowl – it will turn into a thick mixture because of the bran contained in the wholemeal spelt flour – then cover and leave to ferment at room temperature for a couple of hours, then place in the fridge for anything from 12 to 48 hours.

DAY 2
Poolish from Day 1
5g (⅕oz) dried yeast
180g (6⅓oz) water
115g (4oz) sour cream
1 teaspoon black treacle (or use honey, malt syrup, agave syrup)
225g (8oz) strong white flour, plus extra for dusting
225g (8oz) granary flour
9g (³⁄₁₀oz) natural fine salt
25g (1oz) sunflower seeds
25g (1oz) pumpkin seeds

On Day 2, take the poolish out of the fridge a couple of hours before you want to make your bread to allow it to reach room temperature.

In a bowl on a set of scales, start weighing the yeast, then weigh out the water. Remember the importance of the temperature of the water if you're kneading outside the bread machine. Dissolve the yeast in the water. Add the Day 1 poolish to the water and use some of the water to clean the poolish container so you're making the most of that long, flavoursome fermentation.

Add the sour cream and the treacle.

Weigh out the flours straight on top of the water and poolish. Make sure you measure the salt separately for accuracy's sake and place it on top of the flours. Add the seeds towards the end of kneading for them not to interfere with the dough development.

Start the DOUGH programme – the kneading time in a bread machine is usually quite long, at 10–20 minutes, with more kneading involved after a resting period. Stop the programme after that time, remove the dough, restart the programme and return the dough to the pan when the kneading section of the programme is over and it is entering proving mode. If using the machine for proving, regularly check your dough and switch off the machine if you want to prove the loaf for longer.

Alternatively, leave the dough to prove, covered, at room temperature. Either way, proving should normally take between 1 hour and 1 hour 30 minutes.

If you are shaping by hand, transfer the dough to a lightly floured work surface, then go around the dough folding the corners in towards the middle, and turn it over. Cover the dough and give it a bench rest of 10–15 minutes.

After the bench rest is done, turn the dough over on a work surface without flour and fold it tightly towards the centre, going around the dough once. Turn over the dough so the smooth side is up, then place both hands on the side of the loaf and keep rotating it on the same spot until you feel the dough firming up and getting taller.

Place the shaped loaf in the bread machine pan or a proving basket, if you've got one. Let it prove for 1 hour to 1 hour 30 minutes, or until it has doubled in size.

Once you're ready to bake the bread, start the BAKE programme without the bread in the machine, to preheat – about 10 minutes. Lock the pan into the bread machine, spray the inside of the machine with water and bake for 1 hour (you will have to start another BAKE programme to compensate for the preheating time). You might have to carry on with the baking for another 30 minutes to get a little bit more colour on the top of your loaf. Alternatively, use your oven for baking. You can use the bread machine pan in the oven safely, or transfer your loaf to a baking stone or put it on a tray in a hot oven preheated to 250°C, 230°C fan, gas mark 9. Place another baking tray in the base of the oven. Spray the spare baking tray with water when you add the loaf, then bake for 30 minutes, or 40 minutes if you want a nice dark crust.

Remove the baked bread from the oven, leave to cool down for 5 minutes, then carefully take it out of the pan and transfer to a cooling rack. Enjoy still warm or leave it to cool right down before eating.

FERMENTED DOUGH METHOD

DAY 1

100g (3½oz) strong white flour
60g (2oz) water
Pinch of dried yeast

Combine all the ingredients in a small bowl to a rough dough. Transfer to a flourless work surface and mix quickly into a smooth dough – 2–3 minutes is more than enough. Place back in the bowl, cover with cling film, a shower cap, beeswax or a plastic bag and leave to prove at room temperature for 1 hour. Then place it, still covered, in the fridge for 8 to 18 hours before baking – maximum 24 hours.

DAY 2

160g (5½oz) fermented dough
5g (⅕oz) dried yeast
220g (7⅘oz) water
115g (4oz) sour cream
1 teaspoon black treacle (or use honey, malt syrup, agave syrup)
125g (4½oz) strong white flour
100g (3½oz) wholemeal spelt flour
9g (³⁄₁₀oz) natural fine salt
225g (8oz) granary flour
25g (1oz) sunflower seeds
25g (1oz) pumpkin seeds

On Day 2, take the fermented dough out of the fridge a couple of hours before you want to make your bread to allow it to reach room temperature.

In a bowl on a set of scales, start weighing the yeast, then weigh out the water. Remember the importance of the temperature of the water if you're kneading outside the bread machine. Dissolve the yeast in the water. Add the fermented dough to the water. Add the sour cream and the treacle.

Weigh out the flours straight on top of the water and dough. Make sure you measure the salt separately for accuracy's sake and place it on top of the flours. Start the DOUGH programme on your bread machine – the kneading time in a bread machine is usually quite long, at 10-20 minutes, with more kneading involved after a resting period.

Stop the programme after that time, remove the dough, restart the DOUGH programme and return the dough to the pan when the kneading section of the programme is over and it is entering proving mode. If using the machine for proving, regularly check your dough and switch off the machine if you want to prove the loaf for longer. Alternatively, leave the dough to prove, covered, at room temperature. Either way, proving should normally take between 1 hour and 1 hour 30 minutes.

If you are shaping by hand, transfer the dough to a lightly floured work surface, then go around the dough folding the corners in towards the middle, and turn it over. Cover the dough and give it a bench rest of 10–15 minutes.

After the bench rest is done, turn the dough over on a work surface without flour and fold it tightly towards the centre, going around the dough once. Turn over the dough so the smooth side is up, then place both hands on the side of the loaf and keep rotating it on the same spot until you feel the dough firming up and getting taller.

Place the shaped loaf in the bread machine pan or a proving basket, if you've got one. Let it prove for 1 hour to 1 hour 30 minutes, or until it has doubled in size.

Once you're ready to bake the bread, start the BAKE programme without the bread in the machine, to preheat – about 10 minutes. Lock the pan into the bread machine, spray the inside of the machine with water and bake for 1 hour (you will have to start another BAKE programme to compensate for the preheating time). You might have to carry on with the baking for another 30 minutes to get a little bit more colour on the top of your loaf. Alternatively, use your oven for baking. You can use the bread machine pan in the oven safely, or transfer your loaf to a baking stone or put it on a tray in a hot oven preheated to 250°C, 230°C fan, gas mark 9. Place another baking tray in the base of the oven. Spray the spare baking tray with water when you add the loaf, then bake for 30 minutes, or 40 minutes if you want a nice dark crust.

Remove the baked bread from the oven, leave to cool down for 5 minutes, then carefully take it out of the pan and transfer to a cooling rack. Enjoy still warm or leave it to cool right down before eating.

PAIN DE CAMPAGNE

This is a traditional country French loaf that involves usually two types of flour: mainly white with a small quantity of a wholemeal flour – wholemeal wheat, rye or spelt – to give the crumb a speckled effect and the loaf a nice earthy flavour.

POOLISH METHOD

DAY 1
100g (3½oz) strong white flour
100g (3½oz) water
Pinch of dried yeast

Combine all the poolish ingredients together fully in a mixing bowl, cover, and leave to ferment at room temperature for a couple of hours, then place in the fridge for anything from 12 to 48 hours.

DAY 2
Poolish from Day 1
4g (⅕oz) dried yeast
270g (9½oz) water
400g (14oz) strong white flour, plus extra for dusting
60g (2oz) dark or light rye flour (other wholemeal flours can be used)
9g (³⁄₁₀oz) salt

On Day 2, take the poolish out of the fridge a couple of hours before you want to make your bread to allow it to reach room temperature and therefore be ready for action.

In a bowl on a set of scales, start weighing the yeast, then weigh out the water. Remember the importance of the temperature of the water if you're kneading outside the bread machine. Dissolve the yeast in the water. Add the Day 1 poolish to the water and use some of the water to clean the poolish container so you're making the most of that flavoursome fermentation.

Weigh out the flours straight on top of the water and poolish. Make sure you measure the salt separately for accuracy's sake and place it on top of the flours. Start the DOUGH programme on your bread machine – the kneading time in a bread machine is usually quite long, at 10-20 minutes, with more kneading involved after a resting period. I would say that whatever the kneading method you choose, it should be done and dusted in about 6-8 minutes: kneading for longer won't necessarily give you a better dough development.

Stop the programme after that time, remove the dough, restart the DOUGH programme and return the dough to the pan when the kneading section of the programme is over and it is entering proving mode. If using the machine for proving, regularly check your dough and switch off the machine if you want to prove the loaf for longer. Alternatively, leave the dough to prove, covered, at room temperature. Either way, proving should normally take between 1 hour and 1 hour 30 minutes.

If you are shaping by hand, transfer the dough to a lightly floured work surface, then go around the dough

folding the corners in towards the middle, and turn it over. Cover the dough and give it a bench rest of 10–15 minutes.

After the bench rest is done, turn the dough over and fold it tightly towards the centre, going around the dough once. Turn over the dough so the smooth side is up, then place both hands on the side of the loaf and keep rotating it on the same spot until you feel the dough firming up and getting taller.

Place the shaped loaf in the bread machine pan or a proving basket, if you've got one. Let it prove for 1 hour to 1 hour 30 minutes, or until it has doubled in size.

Once you're ready to bake the bread, start the BAKE programme without the bread in the machine, to preheat – about 10 minutes. Lock the pan into the bread machine, spray the inside of the machine with water and bake for 1 hour (you will have to start another BAKE programme to compensate for the preheating time). You might have to carry on with the baking for another 30 minutes to get a little bit more colour on the top of your loaf. Alternatively, use your oven for baking. You can use the bread machine pan in the oven safely, or transfer your loaf to a baking stone or put it on a tray in a hot oven preheated to 250°C, 230°C fan, gas mark 9. Place another baking tray in the base of the oven. Spray the spare baking tray with water when you add

the loaf, then bake for 30 minutes, or 40 minutes if you want a nice dark crust.

Remove the baked bread from the oven, leave to cool down for 5 minutes, then carefully take it out of the pan and transfer to a cooling rack. Enjoy still warm or leave it to cool right down before eating.

FERMENTED DOUGH METHOD

DAY 1
100g (3½oz) strong white flour
60g (2oz) water
Pinch of dried yeast

Combine all the ingredients in a small bowl to a rough dough. Transfer to a flourless work surface and mix quickly into a smooth dough – 2–3 minutes is more than enough. Place back in the bowl, cover with cling film, a shower cap, beeswax or a plastic bag and leave to prove at room temperature for 1 hour. Then place it, still covered, in the fridge for 8 to 18 hours before baking – maximum 24 hours.

DAY 2
160g (5½oz) fermented dough
4g (⅕oz) dried yeast
310g (11oz) water
400g (14oz) strong white flour, plus extra for dusting
60g (2oz) dark or light rye flour
9g (³⁄₁₀oz) natural fine sea salt

On Day 2, take the fermented dough out of the fridge a couple of hours before you want to make your bread to allow it to reach room temperature.

In a bowl on a set of scales, start weighing the yeast, then weigh out the water. Remember the importance of the temperature of the water if you're kneading outside the bread machine. Dissolve the yeast in the water. Add the fermented dough to the water.

Weigh out the flours straight on top of the water and the fermented dough. Make sure you measure the salt separately for accuracy's sake and place it on top of the flours. Start the DOUGH programme on your bread machine – the kneading time in a bread machine is usually quite long, at 10–20 minutes, with more kneading involved after a resting period. I would say that whatever the kneading method you choose, it should be done and dusted in about 6–8 minutes: kneading for longer won't necessarily give you a better dough development.

Stop the programme after that time, remove the dough, restart the programme and return the dough to the pan when the kneading section of the programme is over and it is entering proving mode. If using the machine for proving, regularly check your dough and switch off the machine if you want to prove the loaf for longer. Alternatively, leave the dough to prove, covered, at room temperature. Either way, proving should normally take between 1 hour and 1 hour 30 minutes.

If you are shaping by hand, transfer the dough to a lightly floured work surface, then go around the dough

folding the corners in towards the middle, and turn it over. Don't use an excessive amount of flour while you do this, as it prevents your hands having an effective grasp on the dough: you want the natural stickiness of the dough to help you with the shaping. Cover the dough and give it a bench rest of 10–15 minutes.

After the bench rest is done, turn the dough over on a work surface without flour and fold it tightly towards the centre, going around the dough once. Turn over the dough so the smooth side is up, then place both hands on the side of the loaf and keep rotating it on the same spot until you feel the dough firming up and getting taller.

Once you're ready to bake the bread, start the BAKE programme without the bread in the machine, to preheat – about 10 minutes. Lock the pan into the bread machine, spray the inside of the machine with water and bake for 1 hour (you will have to start another BAKE programme to compensate for the preheating time). You might have to carry on with the baking for another 30 minutes to get a little bit more colour on the top of your loaf. Alternatively, use your oven for baking. You can use the bread machine pan in the oven safely, or transfer your loaf to a baking stone or put it on a tray in a hot oven preheated to 250°C, 230°C fan, gas mark 9. Place another baking tray in the base of the oven. Spray the spare baking tray with water when you add

the loaf, then bake for 30 minutes, or 40 minutes if you want a nice dark crust.

Remove the baked bread from the oven, leave to cool down for 5 minutes, then carefully take it out of the pan and transfer to a cooling rack. Enjoy still warm or leave it to cool right down before eating.

Pre-fermentation: poolish method – the poolish just made, no obvious signs of fermentation yet.

Pre-fermentation: poolish method – poolish is well on its way to being ready to use after a sixteen-hour stay in the fridge.

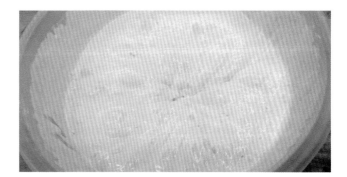

Pre-fermentation: poolish method – close-up of a poolish sagging slightly in the middle indicating fermenation is at its optimum. It's ready to use.

Pre-fermentation: fermented dough process. On the right, the dough has just been mixed. On the left is the fermented version (twelve to twenty-four hours later, after a stay in the fridge) ready to be used.

Folding the dough in the centre with your hand going around the dough once.

The dough looks like a big dumpling with the wrinkly side (the seam) up. Turn it over, seam down against your work surface.

Rotate the dough on the same spot (do not use any flour!) with your hands stuck to the side until it feels firm and is taller than before. It is ready to be put in the pan (seam down).

Brown bread made using overnight cold fermentation in the fridge.

Granary loaf about to be placed in the oven (with the last-minute addition of some sesame seeds found in the cupboard!)

Granary loaf just out of the oven (finding my sesame seeds nicely toasted and making the loaf even more nutritious!).

A nice aerated crumb due to a high hydration. Not bad at all for a wholemeal bread, which can sometimes be quite dense!

Pain de mie rolls tightly shaped, egg-washed and sprinkled with seeds (poppy seeds and linseeds on this occasion).

The *pain de mie* rolls out of the oven!

A tightly shaped brioche placed at the bottom of the pan and waiting to prove.

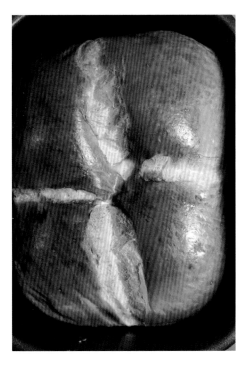

Brioche just out of the oven!

Rye mother culture (starter) having just been fed (refreshed). It is pretty inactive at this stage.

Rye starter ready to use: very active, ascending fermentation.

Proof of a highly active fermentation: a tablespoon of your starter should float in warm water. Your starter is ready for action!

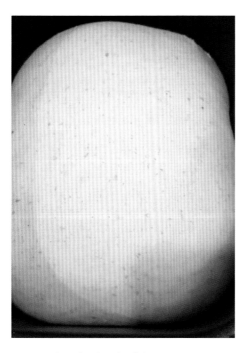

Sourdough white loaf about to go into the oven.

Sourdough white loaf after baking.

A pumpernickel loaf, nice and plump, just before baking.

Pumpernickel loaf after baking – packed with goodness.

CIABATTA

A very popular bread across the world (probably even more than in its home country of Italy!) and loved for its open texture and lightness. Perfect for sandwiches or for making bruschetta when it gets a bit stale. It's a must in your bread making repertoire! Here we're going to give you a loaf version as well as the classic version: the latter not able to be done in a bread machine, of course, but in an oven. This recipe is only using a poolish method (you don't usually use a piece of fermented dough as it is an extremely wet mix where this type of pre-ferment would struggle to be incorporated easily).

POOLISH METHOD

DAY 1
100g (3½oz) strong white flour
100g (3½oz) water
Pinch of dried yeast

Combine all the poolish ingredients together fully in a mixing bowl, cover, and leave to ferment at room temperature for a couple of hours, then place in the fridge for anything from 12 to 48 hours.

DAY 2
Poolish from Day 1
8g (⅓oz) salt
4g (⅕oz) dried yeast
350g (12⅜oz) water
400g (14oz) strong white flour, plus extra for dusting
25g (1oz) extra virgin olive oil

On Day 2, take the poolish out of the fridge a couple of hours before you want to make your bread to allow it to reach room temperature.

In a bowl on a set of scales, start weighing the yeast, then weigh out the water. Remember the importance of the temperature of the water if you're kneading outside the bread machine. Dissolve the yeast in the water. Add the Day 1 poolish to the water and use some of the water to clean the poolish container so you're making the most of that long, flavoursome fermentation.

Weigh out the flour straight on top of the water and poolish. Make sure you measure the salt separately for accuracy's sake and place it on top of the flour. Start the DOUGH programme on your bread machine – the kneading time in a bread machine is usually quite long, at 10–20 minutes, with more kneading involved after a resting period. I would say that whatever the kneading method you choose, it should be done and dusted in about 6–8 minutes: kneading for longer won't necessarily give you a better dough development.

Unlock the pan and transfer the dough to a bowl that has 25g (1oz) of extra virgin olive oil sitting at the bottom. The ciabatta will now need a fold: bring each side of the dough into the middle of the bowl, then turn the piece over, smooth side up. Leave to rest for 45 minutes to 1 hour and repeat the same action three times with the same length of time in between each fold.

If you wish to get ciabatta loaves or panini type buns, generously flour your worktop and deposit the dough onto it 30 minutes after the fourth fold. With a scraper, divide the dough in half, cutting right through it and separating the two loaves by pushing them away from each other so they don't stick back together. If you want ciabatta buns, cut the two dough pieces into quarters or thirds.

For the ciabatta tin, very carefully place the dough at the bottom of the pan, making sure you've got a nice smooth side facing up. Flour the top for a ciabatta effect. Leave the loaf to recover for another 30 to 40 minutes until it rises again.

Place the loaves or buns, stretching them very delicately, onto a lined tray. Give the dough a 15-minute rest, loosely covered with cling film or a plastic bag.

Ciabatta dough being very wet, you are better off baking it in the oven as a tin or loaves or buns. Preheat the oven to 250°C, 230°C fan, gas mark 9, with a baking tray in the base of the oven. Spray the baking tray with water when you add the bread. The dough in the tin will take about 30 minutes to bake, the loaves or buns on a tray around 15 minutes.

ADDING OTHER INGREDIENTS TO A BASIC DOUGH

Don't limit your bread making to just these basic recipes, try tweaking them to suit your creativity and tastes. Enriching a bread with a favourite ingredient is a good starting point! Here are some ideas.

OLIVE BREAD

Use the basic white loaf dough recipe (page 39) or pain de campagne dough recipe (page 79) and add 100g (3½oz) of roughly chopped olives – you can even tear them so they're not too regular. Use black or green – or a mixture of both. If you like, drizzle them with a bit of olive oil and a sprinkle of fresh or dried thyme, rosemary or oregano. Incorporate all these additions towards the end of kneading by adding them to the bread machine, or flatten your dough into a square and scatter them all over, then roll the dough towards you and gently knead until you notice the olives showing all through the dough. Work them in quickly to prevent mashing the olives too much – although, saying that, there's nothing wrong with mixing olive purée with the basic ingredients if you prefer.

Olives also work really well in the ciabatta dough recipe (page 89) – a combination of olive and Cheddar cheese (100g/3½oz of each) is particularly good – then cut the dough into long strips for a delicious snack!

SUN-DRIED TOMATO

Just as you do for olive bread, gently incorporate 100g (3½oz) of roughly chopped marinated sun-dried tomatoes in olive oil and freshly chopped or dried herbs. The ciabatta dough recipe (page 89) is also a good base for the same amount of marinated sun-dried tomatoes.

CHEESE AND PANCETTA BREAD

Gently incorporate 100g (3½oz) cooled fried pancetta cubes – or if you don't have pancetta, bacon lardons work well too – and mix with the same weight of medium-size chunks of Cheddar. Add these ingredients to a basic white loaf (page 39) or pain de campagne dough (page 79).

WALNUT AND RAISIN BREAD

Following the same method as for the olive bread, add 100g (3½oz) each of walnuts and raisins to the dough. This combination makes a version of the classic French rye bread called a benoiton.

BLUE CHEESE AND HAZELNUT BREAD

Add 100g (3½oz) of blue cheese (Roquefort or Dolcelatte type) and 100g (3½oz) of toasted hazelnuts and a drizzle of hazelnut oil to a light rye bread recipe (page 145).

GARLIC BREAD

Add 150g (5¼oz) of roasted garlic marinated in olive oil to a basic white loaf (page 39), pain de campagne (page 79) or ciabatta dough (page 89). These are classic examples of enriched breads, but once again, with my blessing, find your own enrichments to whatever dough you like, just respect the same ratios of 10 to 20% of added ingredients to an amount of dough.

MORNING BREADS

PAIN DE MIE TIN + BURGER BUNS

This could be your basic enriched dough for a tin, burger buns, soft seeded (or not) dinner rolls, hot dog or lobster rolls. This recipe uses a cold fermentation rather than a pre-fermentation but, of course, you could use a poolish or an old dough method (and why not a slow proving overnight in the fridge thrown in for good measure?!).

260g (9oz) water
7g (¼oz) dried yeast
450g (1lb) strong white flour
25g (1oz) full-fat or semi-skimmed powdered milk
18g (⅗oz) sugar
45g (1⅗oz) unsalted butter, softened
9g (³⁄₁₀oz) salt
1 egg, beaten, for the glaze
Seeds, for decoration (optional)

Put in the pan the water and yeast (dissolve the yeast if required). Add the flour, the powdered milk, sugar, the softened butter and the salt (weigh it separately and put it on top of the flour).

Start the DOUGH programme on the bread machine and add the dough mixture. Once the programme has finished, the dough should be fully developed, as for the brioche (page 103). Cover and leave to prove at room temperature for 30 minutes. Fold the dough and place in the fridge for anything from 12 to 18 hours (no pre-ferment is involved this time; the flavour will come from a long cold fermentation).

Remove the dough from the fridge and leave it to come back to room temperature.

If you're making a tin, leave the dough whole, or divide it up if you are making rolls – break it up into 80g (3oz) balls (you can always go for something heavier but 100g (3½oz) would be the maximum weight). Shape, cover and start the bench rest for 10 to 15 minutes.

Shape the dough again according to what you would like to make – a tin or rolls. Leave to prove, covered: for a tin, 45 minutes to 1 hour should be enough; buns will be around 30 to 45 minutes proving time.

Glaze the dough pieces with a beaten egg and sprinkle seeds on top of the buns, if needed. Bake in a pre-heated oven at 200°C, 180°C fan, gas mark 6 – 30 minutes for a tin and 12 to 15 minutes for the buns. If you are using your bread machine for the baking, press the BAKE option, leave it to preheat for 10 minutes, glaze the dough in the tin with egg wash then lower and lock the pan. Carry on with the baking (usually 1 hour), extending the time by restarting the baking cycle once again if more colour is needed. Alternatively, finish under a moderate grill to get the golden-brown colour you would expect on a pain de mie product.

BRIOCHE

A classic French morning treat that has many derivatives, because you can use the dough for myriad products: brioche buns, pain au raisin with pastry cream, enriched brioches with raisins, mixed peels, praline, chocolate chips, nuts, etc. This is so versatile, it's a must for any bread-loving household!

In this recipe, there are two key stages in the dough method: first, making the dough itself, then incorporating the butter. The reason for doing this in two parts is because of the large amount of butter involved in a brioche, and if it was added earlier, it would prevent an effective gluten development, leaving you with a dense and heavy finished product.

6g (⅕oz) dried yeast
25g (1oz) full-fat or semi-skimmed milk, warmed
225g (8oz) beaten eggs
375g (13⅕oz) strong white flour, plus extra for dusting
25g (1oz) sugar
9g (³⁄₁₀oz) natural fine sea salt
185g (6½oz) unsalted butter, softened

First, dissolve the dried yeast in the warm milk and leave it for 5 minutes to activate. Add the eggs to the bread machine pan and add the activated yeast. Weigh the flour on top, then the sugar and salt, weighing the salt on its own for better accuracy.

Put the pan in the bread machine and start the DOUGH programme, following it right to the end to efficiently develop the gluten structure of the dough. When the kneading stops and just before the programme moves to proving, stop the bread machine and give the dough a 5-minute rest for the gluten to relax.

Divide the soft butter into rough quarters and start another DOUGH programme: this time to incorporate the butter. Add the butter a quarter at a time, making sure it is thoroughly mixed into the dough before adding more. The dough should be very soft and very stretchy. Apply the window pane test (page 21).

Take the dough out of the pan, turn it into a ball by folding the dough firmly in the centre and turning it over, then place it in a bowl and cover. Leave it to rise for 1 hour 30 minutes. Degas the dough by taking it out of the bowl, transferring it to a lightly floured work surface and folding the dough towards its centre, rotating the dough each time (basically like turning it into a ball just after kneading).

Place the dough back in the bowl, cover and put it in the fridge for 2 to 3 hours, then repeat the folding as above. Repeat, putting the dough back into the bowl and back in the fridge, this time for a long cold fermentation of a minimum of 8 hours and up to 18 hours maximum.

When ready to bake, take the dough out of the fridge and put it on a lightly floured table. Divide the dough into four portions, or keep it whole for a brioche tin. There's one cardinal rule here: remember that due to the high ratio of fat, handling brioche dough requires careful attention and speed because overmanipulating the dough with warm hands could melt the butter and leave you with a greasy-looking product!

Shape the dough into four equal, tight balls and place them carefully in the pan. Cover very loosely with a lightly oiled piece of cling film and leave to prove for 1 hour 30 minutes to 2 hours, or until it has doubled in size and is almost reaching the rim of the pan. If you want to make a brioche loaf in the tin, just shape the dough into a single tight round ball, place it in the pan and prove for the same length of time. If you want to make delicious brioche buns, divide the dough into 80g (3oz) pieces, brush them with beaten egg and scatter some sugar nibs over them, then prove for about 1 hour.

When the dough has proved, brush with beaten egg again, being very careful not to deflate the risen brioche. Switch on the bread machine to the BAKE programme to preheat for about 10 minutes. Place and lock the pan in the bread machine, spray a little water on the sides of the machine (not on the brioche!) and carry on with the BAKE cycle right to the end. If you need a bit more colour, start the BAKE programme again and check the brioche regularly.

If you are baking in the oven, heat the oven to 200°C, 180°C fan, gas mark 6 and cook the loaf for 20 minutes. Buns will be done in around 12 minutes.

BABKA

Another good thing coming from the East (and even more precisely, from the Eastern European Jewish baking tradition)!

6g (⅕oz) dried yeast

60g (2oz) full-fat milk or semi-skimmed milk

60g (2oz) water

1 large egg, beaten

300g (10½oz) strong white flour, plus extra for dusting

30g (1oz) caster sugar

5g (⅕oz) fine sea salt

75g (2⅝oz) unsalted butter, softened

CHOCOLATE FILLING

50g (1¾oz) unsalted butter

50g (1¾oz) dark cooking chocolate

1 large egg

50g (1¾oz) caster sugar

15g (½oz) cocoa powder

SUGAR GLAZE

100g (3½oz) sugar

80g (2⅘oz) water

Dissolve the yeast in the milk and the water in the bread machine pan, then add the egg. Weigh the flour first then the sugar and salt on top of the liquids and yeast. Start the DOUGH programme. Leave it running until it switches to proving function. Stop the bread machine; the dough at that point can be left alone to relax before incorporating the butter.

Divide the soft butter into rough quarters and start another DOUGH programme. Add the butter a quarter at a time, making sure it is thoroughly mixed into the dough before adding more. The dough should be very soft and very stretchy. Apply the window pane test (page 21).

Take the dough out of the pan, turn it into a ball by folding the dough firmly in the centre and turning it over, then place it in a bowl and cover. Leave it to rise for 1 hour 30 minutes. Degas the dough by taking it out of the bowl, transferring it to a lightly floured table and folding the dough towards its centre, rotating the dough each time (basically like turning it into a ball just after kneading).

Place the dough back in the bowl, cover and put it in the fridge for 2 to 3 hours, then repeat the folding as above. Repeat, putting the dough back into the bowl and back in the fridge, this time for a long cold fermentation of a minimum of 8 hours and up to 18 hours maximum.

First rise over, take the dough out and leave it for about 1 hour to return to room temperature. In the meantime, prepare the chocolate filling. First, melt the butter and chocolate together in a metallic bowl over a pan of boiling water. In another bowl, combine the egg, sugar and cocoa powder until it becomes very creamy and smooth. Add the melted butter and chocolate to the cocoa powder mixture and whisk together. Set aside – don't let it go totally cold, as the filling could set hard and not spread easily.

Dust your worktop lightly with flour and turn out the babka dough onto it. Sprinkle a bit more flour on top, then place your rolling pin at the centre of the dough and start extending it to a 45cm (18in) length, then give your dough a quarter of a turn towards you and start rolling it out again to the same length. You should end up with a 45cm (18in) square piece of dough, 3mm thick.

Spread the filling all over the square, leaving a small band of dough at the bottom edge. Lightly wet that band and start rolling the dough towards you, tightly, until it resembles a log. Cut the log lengthways with a knife and turn the dough on its side so the chocolatey layers are facing up. Twist the two newly created sides together into a very simple plait. Place the babka in the pan (you'll have to press it gently like an accordion to make it fit, but that's absolutely fine).

Cover with a very loose, slightly oiled piece of cling film and leave to prove for 1 hour 30 minutes to 2 hours.

When proved, put on the BAKE programme and leave it to preheat for 10 minutes before placing the babka in the tin into the bread machine and locking the pan.

There's no need for eggwash, the babka will be glazed later after baking. If baking the babka in the oven, put the pan into an oven preheated to 200°C, 180°C fan, gas mark 6 with a baking tray in the base of the oven. Spray the baking tray with water when you add the babka, then bake 25 minutes.

While the babka is baking, make the glaze by bringing the sugar and water together to the boil in a pan and leaving to simmer for 2 or 3 minutes to make thick and sticky. When the babka has finished baking, take it out of the pan and brush straightaway with the glaze.

Enjoy the babka while it's still warm!

ANCIENT GRAINS

Ancient grains are going to give you a truly wholemeal loaf with flours that haven't been overly modified and interfered with like modern wheat. If you're after a nutritious, healthy, very tasty and genuine back-to-the-roots type of bread, those flours are yours to play around with. Just remember that they can be difficult to work with, as their gluten is weaker and more water soluble than that in strong white flour, and for that very reason they tend to lack in volume and be on the dense side. I don't think mixing them with some strong white flour or even adding a certain amount of pure gluten is blasphemous. Again, you're the master of your own baking destiny, if you want to use them straight with no white flour addition, why not?!

LIGHT SPELT TIN

POOLISH METHOD
100g (3½oz) white spelt
100g (3½oz) water
Pinch of dried yeast

DAY 1
Combine all the poolish ingredients together fully in a mixing bowl, cover, and leave to ferment at room temperature for a couple of hours, then place in the fridge for anything from 12 to 48 hours.

DAY 2
Poolish from Day 1
5g (⅕oz) dried yeast
265g (9³⁄₁₀oz) water
450g (1lb) white spelt flour, plus extra for dusting
1 teaspoon agave syrup
9g (³⁄₁₀oz) salt

On Day 2, take the poolish out of the fridge a couple of hours before you want to make your bread to allow it to reach room temperature.

In a bowl on a set of scales, start weighing the yeast, then weigh out the water. Remember the importance of the temperature of the water if you're kneading outside the bread machine. Dissolve the yeast in the water. Add the Day 1 poolish to the water and use some of the water to clean the poolish container so you're making the most of that long, flavoursome fermentation.

Weigh out the flours straight on top of the water and poolish. Make sure you measure the salt separately for accuracy's sake and place it on top of the flours. Start the DOUGH programme on your bread machine – the kneading time in a bread machine is usually quite long, at 10–20 minutes, with more kneading involved after a resting period. I would say that whatever the kneading method you choose, it should be done and dusted in about 6–8 minutes: kneading for longer won't necessarily give you a better dough development.

Stop the programme after that time, remove the dough, restart the programme and return the dough to the pan when the kneading section of the programme is over and it is entering proving mode. If using the machine for proving, regularly check your dough and switch off the machine if you want to prove the loaf for longer. Alternatively, leave the dough to prove, covered, at room temperature. Either way, proving should normally take between 1 hour and 1 hour 30 minutes.

If you are shaping by hand, transfer the dough to a lightly floured work surface, then go around the dough folding the corners in towards the middle, and turn it over. Cover the dough and give it a bench rest of 10–15 minutes.

After the bench rest is done, turn the dough over on a work surface without flour and fold it tightly towards the centre, going around the dough once. Turn over the dough so the smooth side is up, then place both hands on the side of the loaf and keep rotating it on the same spot until you feel the dough firming up and getting taller.

Place the shaped loaf in the pan or a proving basket, if you've got one. Let it prove for 1 hour to 1 hour 30 minutes or until it has doubled in size.

Once you're ready to bake the bread, start the BAKE programme without the bread in the machine, to preheat – about 10 minutes. Lock the pan into the bread machine, spray the inside of the machine with water and bake for 1 hour (you will have to start another BAKE programme to compensate for the preheating time). You might have to carry on with the baking for another 30 minutes to get a little bit more colour on the top of your loaf. Alternatively, use your oven for baking. You can use the bread machine pan in the oven safely, or transfer your loaf to a baking stone or put it on a tray in a hot oven preheated to 250°C, 230°C fan, gas mark 9. Place another baking tray in the base of the oven. Spray the spare baking tray with water when you add the loaf, then bake for 30 minutes, or 40 minutes if you want a nice dark crust.

Remove the baked bread from the oven, leave to cool down for 5 minutes, then carefully take it out of the pan and transfer to a cooling rack. Enjoy still warm or leave it to cool right down before eating.

WHOLEMEAL SPELT

POOLISH METHOD
100g (3½oz) strong white flour
100g (3½oz) water
Pinch of dried yeast

DAY 1
Combine all the poolish ingredients together fully in a mixing bowl, cover, and leave to ferment at room temperature for a couple of hours, then place in the fridge for anything from 12 to 48 hours.

DAY 2
Poolish from Day 1
4g (⅕oz) dried yeast
270g (9½oz) water
200g (7oz) strong white flour, plus extra for dusting
250g (8⅞oz) wholemeal spelt
9g (³⁄₁₀oz) natural fine sea salt

On Day 2, take the poolish out of the fridge a couple of hours before you want to make your bread to allow it to reach room temperature.

In a bowl on a set of scales, start weighing the yeast, then weigh out the water. Dissolve the yeast in the water. Add the poolish to the water and use some of the water to clean the poolish container so you're making the most of that flavoursome fermentation.

Weigh out the flours straight on top of the water and poolish. Make sure you measure the salt separately for accuracy's sake and place it on top of the flours. Start the DOUGH programme on your bread machine – the kneading time in a bread machine is usually quite long, at 10–20 minutes, with more kneading involved after a resting period. I would say that whatever the kneading method you choose, it should be done and dusted in about 6–8 minutes: kneading for longer won't necessarily give you a better dough development.

Stop the programme after that time, remove the dough, restart the DOUGH programme and return the dough to the pan when the kneading section of the programme is over and it is entering proving mode. If using the machine for proving, regularly check your dough and switch off the machine if you want to prove the loaf for longer. Alternatively, leave the dough to prove, covered, at room temperature. Either way, proving should normally take between 1 hour and 1 hour 30 minutes.

If you are shaping by hand, transfer the dough to a lightly floured work surface, then go around the dough folding the corners in towards the middle, and turn it over. Cover the dough and give it a bench rest of 10–15 minutes.

After the bench rest is done, turn the dough over on a work surface without flour and fold it tightly towards the centre, going around the dough once. Turn over the dough so the smooth side is up, then place both hands on the side of the loaf and keep rotating it on the same spot until you feel the dough firming up and getting taller.

Place the shaped loaf in the bread machine pan or a proving basket, if you've got one. Let it prove for 1 hour to 1 hour 30 minutes, or until it has doubled in size.

Once you're ready to bake the bread, start the BAKE programme without the bread in the machine, to preheat – about 10 minutes. Lock the pan into the bread machine, spray the inside of the machine with water and bake for 1 hour (you will have to start another BAKE programme to compensate for the preheating time). You might have to carry on with the baking for another 30 minutes to get a little bit more colour on the top of your loaf. Alternatively, use your oven for baking. You can use the bread machine pan in the oven safely, or transfer your loaf to a baking stone or put it on a tray in a hot oven preheated to 250°C, 230°C fan, gas mark 9. Place another baking tray in the base of the oven. Spray the spare baking tray with water when you add the loaf, then bake for 30 minutes, or 40 minutes if you want a nice dark crust.

Remove the baked bread from the oven, leave to cool down for 5 minutes, then carefully take it out of the pan and transfer to a cooling rack. Enjoy still warm or leave it to cool right down before eating.

FERMENTED DOUGH METHOD

DAY 1
100g (3½oz) strong white flour
60g (2oz) water
Pinch of dried yeast

Mix all the Day 1 ingredients in a small bowl to obtain a rough dough. Transfer it to a flourless table and mix quickly into a smooth dough – 2 to 3 minutes is more than enough. Place back in the bowl, cover with cling film, a shower cap, beeswax or a plastic bag, and leave to prove at room temperature for 1 hour. Then place it, still covered, in the fridge for 8 to 18 hours before baking – maximum 24 hours.

DAY 2
160g (5½oz) fermented dough
4g (⅕oz) dried yeast
310g (11oz) water
200g (7oz) strong white flour, plus extra for dusting
250g (8⅞oz) wholemeal spelt
9g (³⁄₁₀oz) natural fine sea salt

On Day 2, take the fermented dough out of the fridge a couple of hours before you want to make your bread to allow it to reach room temperature.

In a bowl on a set of scales, start weighing the yeast, then weigh out the water. Remember the importance of the temperature of the water if you're kneading outside the bread machine. Dissolve the yeast in the water. Add the fermented dough to the water.

Weigh out the flours straight on top of the water and the fermented dough. Make sure you measure the salt separately for accuracy's sake and place it on top of the flours. Start the DOUGH programme on your bread machine – the kneading time in a bread machine is usually quite long, at 10–20 minutes, with more kneading involved after a resting period. I would say that whatever the kneading method you choose, it should be done and dusted in about 6–8 minutes: kneading for longer won't necessarily give you a better dough development.

Stop the programme after that time, remove the dough, restart the DOUGH programme and return the dough to the pan when the kneading section of the programme is over and it is entering proving mode. If using the machine for proving, regularly check your dough and switch off the machine if you want to prove the loaf for longer. Alternatively, leave the dough to prove, covered, at room temperature. Either way, proving should normally take between 1 hour and 1 hour 30 minutes.

If you are shaping by hand, transfer the dough to a lightly floured work surface, then go around the dough

folding the corners in towards the middle, and turn it over. Cover the dough and give it a bench rest of 10–15 minutes.

After the bench rest is done, turn the dough over on a work surface without flour and fold it tightly towards the centre, going around the dough once. Turn over the dough so the smooth side is up, then place both hands on the side of the loaf and keep rotating it on the same spot until you feel the dough firming up and getting taller.

Place the shaped loaf in the bread machine pan or a proving basket, if you've got one. Let it prove for 1 hour to 1 hour 30 minutes, or until it has doubled in size.

Once you're ready to bake the bread, start the BAKE programme without the bread in the machine, to preheat – about 10 minutes. Lock the pan into the bread machine, spray the inside of the machine with water and bake for 1 hour (you will have to start another BAKE programme to compensate for the preheating time). You might have to carry on with the baking for another 30 minutes to get a little bit more colour on the top of your loaf. Alternatively, use your oven for baking. You can use the bread machine pan in the oven safely, or transfer your loaf to a baking stone or tray in an oven preheated to 250°C, 230°C fan, gas mark 9. Place another baking tray in the base of the oven. Spray the spare baking tray with water when you add the loaf, then bake for 30 minutes, or 40 minutes if you want a nice dark crust.

Remove the baked bread from the oven, leave to cool down for 5 minutes, then carefully take it out of the pan and transfer to a cooling rack. Enjoy still warm or leave it to cool right down before eating.

EINKORN, SPELT AND KHORASAN BREAD

Three ancient grains in one loaf for a great tasting experience. This will only use a poolish method using the very granular einkorn flour for the pre-fermentation stage. Gluten is added to the Day 2 ingredients to improve the texture of the loaf, but this is optional; Vital gluten is a brand that is available online or in health food shops.

EINKORN POOLISH

100g (3½oz) einkorn flour
100g (3½oz) water
Pinch of dried yeast

DAY 1
Combine all the poolish ingredients together fully in a mixing bowl, cover, and leave to ferment at room temperature for a couple of hours, then place in the fridge for anything from 12 to 48 hours.

DAY 2
Poolish from Day 1
4g (⅕oz) dried yeast
275g (9⁷⁄₁₀oz) water
300g (10½oz) white spelt flour, plus extra for dusting
150g (5¼oz) Khorasan flour
10g (⅓oz) dried gluten (optional)
9g (³⁄₁₀oz) natural fine sea salt

On Day 2, take the poolish out of the fridge a couple of hours before you want to make your bread to allow it to reach room temperature.

In a bowl on a set of scales, start weighing the yeast, then weigh out the water. Remember the importance of the temperature of the water if you're kneading outside the bread machine. Dissolve the yeast in the water. Add the Day 1 poolish to the water and use some of the water to clean the poolish container so you're making the most of that flavoursome fermentation.

Weigh out the flours straight on top of the water and poolish. Make sure you measure the salt separately for accuracy's sake and place it on top of the flours. Start the DOUGH programme on your bread machine – the kneading time in a bread machine is usually quite long, at 10–20 minutes, with more kneading involved after a resting period. I would say that whatever the kneading method you choose, it should be done and dusted in about 6–8 minutes: kneading for longer won't necessarily give you a better dough development.

Stop the programme after that time, remove the dough, restart the DOUGH programme and return the dough to the pan when the kneading section of the programme is over and it is entering proving mode. If using the machine for proving, regularly check your dough and switch off the machine if you want to prove the loaf for longer. Alternatively, leave the dough to prove, covered, at room temperature. Either way, proving should normally take between 1 hour and 1 hour 30 minutes.

If you are shaping by hand, transfer the dough to a lightly floured work surface, then go around the dough folding the corners in towards the middle, and turn it over. Cover the dough and give it a bench rest of 10–15 minutes.

After the bench rest is done, turn the dough over and fold it tightly towards the centre, going around the dough once. Turn over the dough so the smooth side is up, then place both hands on the side of the loaf and keep rotating it on the same spot until you feel the dough firming up and getting taller.

Place the shaped loaf in the bread machine pan or a proving basket, if you've got one. Let it prove for 1 hour to 1 hour 30 minutes, or until it has doubled in size.

Once you're ready to bake the bread, start the BAKE programme without the bread in the machine, to preheat – about 10 minutes. Lock the pan into the bread machine, spray the inside of the machine with water and bake for 1 hour (you will have to start another BAKE programme to compensate for the preheating time). You might have to carry on with the baking for another 30 minutes to get a little bit more colour on the top of your loaf. Alternatively, use your oven for baking. You can use the bread machine pan in the oven safely, or transfer your loaf to a baking stone or put it on a tray in a hot oven preheated to 250°C, 230°C fan, gas mark 9. Place another baking tray in the base of the oven. Spray the spare baking tray with water when you add the loaf, then bake for 30 minutes, or 40 minutes if you want a nice dark crust.

Remove the baked bread from the oven, leave to cool down for 5 minutes, then carefully take it out of the pan and transfer to a cooling rack. Enjoy still warm or leave it to cool right down before eating.

SOURDOUGH BREADS

Yes, you can make proper sourdough in a bread machine! I thought it would be absolutely necessary to write a section on sourdough breads and introduce bread machine users to naturally leavened loaves.

By now, you should be aware of pre-fermentations and long rises in the fridge as part of the bread making method, and sourdough breads need similar care. You can use your bread machine for the mixing of the dough but it's better to do the rest of the process by hand. I would always bake the loaf in the domestic oven, as it will do your long-awaited loaf full justice! In a sourdough loaf, you definitely want a pronounced dark crust because a soft underbaked crust is not going to be satisfactory at all – far too soft to be fully enjoyable.

In the sourdough process, the first step is to create your own yeast by simply harvesting and harnessing surrounding wild yeasts and bacteria floating about in your environment. The process is a fascinating one: from some flour and water mixed together, you're progressively observing life emerging and going from strength to strength – that's a powerful feeling of genuine amazement and pride! Of course, the unique taste of a sourdough loaf also explains the ever-growing attraction to sourdough baking.

Let's start with making our mother culture, the beginning of all things sourdough.

MAKING THE STARTER

Soak 100g (3½oz) of wheat bran in 400g (14oz) of water and leave overnight at room temperature. The following day, filter the water through a sieve so the bran is left behind, but keep the water and use it for the first feed.

FEED ONE

50g (1¾oz) rye flour
50g (1¾oz) reserved water

Mix the rye flour and water into a thick paste. Cover with a damp cloth and leave at room temperature if it's warm enough in your kitchen; if not, make sure it is left in a warm spot somewhere in your home. This step is about promoting fermentation, which is at its best at around 24–25°C (75–77°F).

Repeat the same operation with the same quantities for the next 5 days, with a 24-hour gap between feeds (choose the feeding time to accommodate your daily activities; for example, 7am or 7pm could be a good time). It requires a bit of discipline, but nothing too drastic!

When the 6 days have elapsed, you should be getting a very active starter that's ready for action. At that point, place it in the fridge to avoid over-fermentation and to keep a healthy balance between bacterial and yeast activities. You can keep it in the fridge, idle, for 3 weeks without risking losing your starter, bearing in mind the more you're using it, the more vigorous and consistent it will be.

Refresh the starter 8 to 12 hours before in order to work with a peaking fermentation, not a tired and deflated one. The idea is to refresh with what you'll need for a specific recipe; for example, for the pumpernickel recipe you want 160g (5½oz) of refreshed starter, meaning you're going to add 80g (2⅘oz) of each flour and water on top of the starter, mix them together thoroughly and place it back in the fridge. Next day, take your 160g (5½oz) of peaking starter. No accumulation, no discard – very straightforward!

PUMPERNICKEL

160g (5½oz) rye starter
450g (1lb) warm water
350g (12³⁄₁₀oz) light rye flour
70g (2½oz) dark rye flour
100g (3½oz) sunflower seeds
100g (3½oz) pumpkin seeds
9g (³⁄₁₀oz) natural fine sea salt
Sunflower, sesame, linseed, chia or poppy seeds, to sprinkle

Refresh your starter the day before. Leave it in the fridge overnight.

Take your refreshed starter out of the fridge. Transfer 160g (5½oz) of your starter to the pan and place the mother culture straight back into the fridge. Leave the 160g (5½oz) of starter at room temperature for it to become increasingly active. Add the warm water (this will speed up the fermentation, helping it to lift a noticeably dense dough).

Switch on the DOUGH programme and place the dough in the bread machine. At the end of the knead-ing setting, make sure the dough is levelled by using your scraper dipped in a bit of water to take any stuck rye batter from the sides of the pan. Leave the dough to rise in the bread machine until the dough is inching towards the top of the pan – this should take about 2 to 3 hours in your kitchen.

Carefully unlock the pan and remove it from the bread machine (if easier, just leave the dough to prove loosely covered at room temperature). Place the pan in a preheated oven at 220°C, 200°C fan, gas mark 7, which has a baking tray placed in the base. Bake for 1 hour, occasionally spraying the baking tray with water.

WHITE SOURDOUGH LOAF

160g (5½oz) rye starter
320g (11⅓oz) water
500g (1lb 2oz) strong white flour
10g (⅓oz) natural fine sea salt

Take your refreshed starter out of the fridge. Transfer 160g (5½oz) of your starter to the pan and place the mother culture straight back into the fridge. Leave the 160g (5½oz) of starter at room temperature for it to become increasingly active. Add the warm water.

Switch on the DOUGH programme and place the dough in the bread machine. When the RISE function kicks in, switch off the machine, take the pan out of the bread machine, cover with a shower cap or plastic bag and leave at room temperature for 4 to 5 hours, giving the dough a fold after 3 hours – firmly fold the dough towards the centre as you're rotating it at the same time, then turn the dough over smooth side up.

After the first rise, take the dough out of the pan and preshape loosely into a round loaf, then give it a 15-minute bench rest.

After the bench rest is done, turn the dough over and fold it tightly towards the centre, going around the dough once. Turn over the dough so the smooth side is up, then place both hands on the side of the loaf and keep rotating it on the same spot until you feel the dough firming up and getting taller.

Place it back in the pan, or if you are using a proving basket, place your loaf upside down (seam up), cover and leave to prove for between 2 and 3 hours or until doubled in size.

If you are using a proving basket, turn it over so the loaf stands the right way up on a baking tray or a wooden peel (to be slid onto a baking stone like a pizza), or just bake in the pan in a preheated oven at 250°C, 230°C fan, gas 9 for 30–40 minutes until you get a nice dark crust.

WHOLEMEAL SOURDOUGH

160g (5½oz) rye starter
200g (7oz) strong wholemeal flour
50g (1¾oz) wholemeal spelt
250g (8⅞oz) strong white flour
350g (12³⁄₁₀oz) water
10g (⅓oz) salt

Take your refreshed starter out of the fridge. Transfer 160g (5½oz) of your starter to the pan and place the mother culture straight back in the fridge. Leave the 160g (5½oz) of starter at room temperature for it to become increasingly active. Add the water.

Switch on the DOUGH programme and place the dough in the bread machine. When the RISE function kicks in, switch off the machine, take the pan out of the bread machine and cover with a shower cap or plastic bag and leave at room temperature for 4 to 5 hours, giving the dough a fold after 3 hours – firmly fold the dough towards the centre as you're rotating it at the same time, then turn the dough over smooth side up.

After the first rise, take the dough out of the pan and preshape it loosely into a round loaf, then give it a 15-minute bench rest.

After the bench rest is done, turn the dough over and fold it tightly towards the centre, going around the dough once. Turn over the dough so the smooth side is up, then place both hands on the side of the loaf and keep rotating it on the same spot until you feel the dough firming up and getting taller.

Place it back in the pan, or if you are using a proving basket, place your loaf upside down (seam up), cover and leave to prove for between 2 and 3 hours or until doubled in size.

If you are using a proving basket, turn it over so the loaf stands the right way up on a baking tray or a wooden peel (to be slid onto a baking stone like a pizza), or just bake in the pan in a preheated oven at 250°C, 230°C fan, gas 9 with a baking tray in the base of the oven. Spray the baking tray with water when you add the loaf, then bake for 30–40 minutes until you get a nice dark crust.

RYE SOURDOUGH

160g (5½oz) rye starter
350g (12³⁄₁₀oz) water
400g (14oz) strong white flour
120g (4⅕oz) light rye flour
11g (⅖oz) natural fine sea salt

Take your refreshed starter out of the fridge. Transfer 160g (5½oz) of your starter to the pan and place the mother culture straight back in the fridge. Leave the 160g (5½oz) of starter at room temperature for it to become increasingly active. Add the water.

Switch on the DOUGH programme and place the dough in the bread machine. When the RISE function kicks in, switch off the machine, take the pan out of the bread machine and cover with a shower cap or plastic bag and leave at room temperature for 4 to 5 hours, giving the dough a fold after 3 hours – firmly fold the dough towards the centre as you're rotating it at the same time, then turn the dough over smooth side up.

After the first rise, take the dough out of the pan and preshape it loosely into a round loaf, then give it a 15-minute bench rest.

After the bench rest is done, turn the dough over and fold it tightly towards the centre, going around the dough once. Turn over the dough so the smooth side is up, then place both hands on the side of the loaf and keep rotating it on the same spot until you feel the dough firming up and getting taller.

Place it back in the pan, or if you are using a proving basket, place your loaf upside down (seam up), cover and leave to prove for between 2 and 3 hours or until doubled in size.

If you are using a proving basket, turn it over so the loaf stands the right way up on a baking tray or a wooden peel (to be slid onto a baking stone like a pizza), or just bake in the pan in a preheated oven at 250°C, 230°C fan, gas 9 with a baking tray in the base of the oven. Spray the baking tray with water when you add the loaf, then bake for 30–40 minutes until you get a nice dark crust.

SOURDOUGH BUCKWHEAT

Unusual sourdough but a great-tasting one with solely the use of flour (excluding the small amount of rye flour contained in your natural starter).

160g (5½oz) rye starter
200g (7oz) strong white flour
240g (8½oz) buckwheat flour
10g (⅓oz) Vital gluten
290g (10⅕oz) water
9g (³⁄₁₀oz) natural fine sea salt

Take your refreshed starter out of the fridge. Transfer 160g (5½oz) of your starter to the pan and place the mother culture straight back in the fridge. Leave the 160g (5½oz) of starter at room temperature for it to become increasingly active. Add the water.

Switch on the DOUGH programme and place the dough in the bread machine. When the RISE function kicks in, switch off the machine, take the pan out of the bread machine and cover with a shower cap or plastic bag and leave at room temperature for 4 to 5 hours, giving the dough a fold – firmly fold the dough towards the centre as you're rotating it at the same time, then turn the dough over smooth side up.

After the first rise, take the dough out of the pan and preshape it loosely into a round loaf, then give it a 15-minute bench rest.

After the bench rest is done, turn the dough over and fold it tightly towards the centre, going around the dough once. Turn over the dough so the smooth side is up, then place both hands on the side of the loaf and keep rotating it on the same spot until you feel the dough firming up and getting taller.

Place it back in the pan, or if you are using a proving basket, place your loaf upside down (seam up), cover and leave to prove for between 2 and 3 hours or until doubled in size.

If you are using a proving basket, turn it over so the loaf stands the right way up on a baking tray or a wooden peel (to be slid onto a baking stone like a pizza), or just bake in the pan in a preheated oven at 250°C, 230°C fan, gas 9 with a baking tray in the base of the oven. Spray the baking tray with water when you add the loaf, then bake for 30–40 minutes until you get a nice dark crust.

PASTRY DOUGHS

Why not use your bread machine to make basic pastry doughs and batters? Here are some recipes you may find useful and easy to put together. The recipes here make enough dough to have some put away in the freezer for later use.

SHORTCRUST PASTRY

250g (8⅞oz) unsalted butter, softened
500g (1lb 2oz) plain flour
10g (⅓oz) natural fine sea salt
75g (2⅝oz) cold water
2 medium eggs, lightly beaten

Place the butter between two small sheets of baking parchment and roll with a rolling pin until soft. Weigh the flour into the pan, then add the softened butter and the salt (weighed separately).

Switch on the DOUGH programme and mix until the butter is almost fully combined in the flour. Add the water and beaten eggs and carry on mixing until you get a smooth dough. Don't over-knead or you will end up with a tough dough that's not brittle enough for a good pastry.

Divide the dough in half (or even into thirds if you own a medium-size flan tin), wrap in cling film and put in your freezer until ready to use. Defrost overnight in the fridge and roll while still slightly cool.

SWEET PASTRY

300g (10½oz) unsalted butter, softened
500g (1lb 2oz) plain flour
2g (⅒oz) natural fine sea salt
125g (4½oz) caster sugar
3 medium eggs

Place the butter between two small sheets of baking parchment and roll with a rolling pin until soft. Weigh the flour into the pan, then add the softened butter.

Switch on the DOUGH programme and mix until the butter is almost fully combined in the flour. Add the salt, sugar and beaten eggs and carry on mixing until you get a smooth dough. Don't over-knead or you will end up with a tough dough that's not brittle enough for a good pastry.

Divide the dough in half (or even into thirds if you own a medium-size flan tin), wrap in cling film and put in your freezer until ready to use. Defrost overnight in the fridge and roll while still slightly cool.

Thoughts About an Improved Bread Machine Design

As I was trialling recipes for this book and comparing my extensive artisan baking background with my recent experience in using a bread machine, I was questioning what my 'perfect' bread machine would be like. Even if at first I was alien to the process and probably prejudiced against it, the journey has been an eye-opening one, and I soon started to understand why such baking equipment may be attractive to the wider public and that I shouldn't be judgemental about it.

As I mentioned at the beginning of the book, a bread machine user may have a genuine dislike of the mess involved in making a loaf, or may be looking at eating better bread without being overly interested in the process (but actually may be more involved with that process later on by switching to hand kneading, for instance) or, of course, may be suffering from a medical condition or even a disability that prevents them from using their hands for baking – all those people still have the right to make their own bread!

But this said, it is at a design level that I have some reservations about bread machines, and I would suggest that there is room for improvement. My main concerns are not much around the kneading but more around the proving and baking stages.

I noticed pretty soon that the way a bread machine typically works limits its use to only a short fermentation method, when we know that good bread benefits enormously from a longer fermentation. The design of the bread machine revolves around straight doughs that rely on a relatively high amount of yeast (and the addition of sugar to activate that yeast).

The kneading already warms up the dough quite significantly, and then the heating element kicks in to initiate the proving and speed up the rise. There is no control of the temperature, and it seems quite warm. No added moisture is present during proving, which means that a drier environment can crust the dough in return: yeast loves warmth but also humidity.

If I were to design a bread machine, my recommendations for a better proving would be to guarantee a constant proving temperature at around 24 or 25°C (75 or 77°F) in the inner chamber, and the installation of a humidifier at the bottom of the machine. For a home baker, doing the long proof by placing the pan in the fridge is the simplest and most straightforward solution that does not involve any change in design.

The baking definitely could be improved. What really took me aback is the almost near impossibility to get some serious colours on the loaf, specifically on top of it (the sides of the bread are actually not bad at all after baking), leaving it very soft and visually unattractive. Brushing the loaf with egg wash or light syrup to help with the coloration seems a very poor way out...

The bread machines can't achieve the high temperature (230–250°C/446–482°F) required for bread baking and they don't have any steam injection, which is so crucial for a good caramelisation of the crust. How could we remedy this? My first thoughts would be to see if the Dutch oven method could be used: trapping the loaf in a closed pan rather than baking it in an open one would resolve the issue of insufficient steam production – the bread would simply steam itself, which would help with the volume of the loaf, too. Removing the lid of the pan towards the end of baking would help to dry and colour the crust further. Integrating a heating element into the lid of the machine (the viewing window would have to be removed from the usual design) to create a source of heat from the top (and not only from the sides, as it is currently) would also help, as it would concentrate the heat on the top part of the loaf.

I'm no technician, of course, but would those changes be that difficult to incorporate into the design of a new generation of bread machines? They would greatly improve the quality of the bread produced. I'll leave it to the problem-solving engineers out there to answer that question!

Epilogue

This is it; it's all down to you from now on...

I truly hope you found this book engaging enough to inspire you to use your newly acquired bread machine more often, or just to change the way you've been using it so far to get even better loaves from it.

Made by hand or in a bread machine, the loaf you produce is above all one that you've created – and you should be pretty chuffed about that! This book is more for guidance and nurturing general interest in baking – I will never claim that it is the ultimate recipe book that one should follow religiously! So, as I always say, don't hesitate to change the recipes and tweak them to be the way you want them: you may choose to add more or less water, more or less yeast, more or less proving time, for instance, because it works better for you and to produce the kind of bread that you like to eat. Experimenting is the key to success – some loaves may fail abysmally but you'll learn immensely from those mistakes. Others might be a resounding success, on the other hand, and if that success repeats itself consistently, you'll know that you're a stage further in your very own bread journey!

There is a lot to learn from artisan bread in terms of baking techniques and quality (both in taste and appearance) of the end product. But, as I discovered in the process of writing this book, the learning and experimenting I did hasn't been a one-way affair; far from it, I tremendously enjoyed 'playing around' with my bread machine. At a personal level, I can honestly say that it has been as much an eye opener for me as I hope this book will be for you. It's inspired me to think about other unusual and labour-saving ways to bake bread, too, so much so that I've even started experimenting with a slow cooker. That's a work in progress, but I have had some great results already with rye pumpernickel types of breads, which are actually in their element when baked for a long period of time in constant steam, and my bao buns were pretty good too!

Unequivocally, I've concluded that you *can* produce excellent loaves out of your bread machine, and that far from being solely a convenient, practical piece of equipment, it can be a useful tool with a real purpose – not a short-lived gadget soon gathering dust in the farthest corner of your kitchen but very much an eagerly anticipated occasion and even a regularly used and hard-working appliance.

So, enjoy your bread machine and fill your kitchen with the aroma of freshly baked bread!

Acknowledgements

I am grateful to Duncan Proudfoot of Palazzo Editions for giving me the opportunity to write another baking-related book. I would like to make special mention of Helena Caldon for taking on the essential task of editing the manuscript.

A very warm thank-you also to Elizabeth Marcellin for her unabated support and patience as ever and my heartfelt apologies for disappearing in front of my computer for long periods of time during the writing of this book. I must mention my friend Dave Newman for very kindly lending me an extra bread machine and for not holding a grudge for still not having returned it to him nearly a year later!

Finally I'd like to thank Bread Ahead bakery school for allowing me to hone my skills as a teacher, helping so many enthusiastic students on their bread journey.